Other Books by Tony Seton

Long Short Fiction Truth
The Larger Reality / The Realm of Higher Consciousness
Do You Mind?
The Ultimate App
Covid Blue
Thought So
True Tens / Seven Women of Beautiful Character
The Flight of KAL 007
Silent Alarm
Truth Be Told
Mayhem
Jennifer
The Francie LeVillard Mysteries - Volumes I- XI
The Francie LeVillard Mysteries - The Early Years
Just Imagine
Trinidad Head
Deki-san
Equinox
Mokki's Peak
No Soap, Radio
Paradise Pond
The Autobiography of John Dough, Gigolo
Silver Lining
The Omega Crystal/New Moves
Musings on Sherlock Holmes
Say It Write
Is There a Why?
13 Days of Fear
Selected Writings
The Brink
Dead as a Doorbell
The Quality Interview / Getting It Right
   on Both Sides of the Mic
From Terror to Triumph /
   The Herma Smith Curtis Story
Don't Mess with the Press / How to Write,
   Produce, and Report Quality Television News
Right Car, Right Price

The Bright Wise Solution

The Bright Wise Solution

A novel by Tony Seton

Carmel, California

April 2025

This is a novel. However, it is based on considerable research about the crises that have befallen our educational system. While statistics may be open to interpretation and dispute, most of those cited in these pages are from legitimate sources and at least close to accurate. The characters in this book are fictional, except those expressly cited via historical reference.

The Bright Wise Solution

All Rights Reserved

© 2018 by Tony Seton

Thank you to Susan Jacoby for the use of a sentence from page 53 of her very important book, *The Age of American Unreason* (Pantheon Books 2008).

Thank you also to my esteemed friend, the brilliant Rebecca Costa, for use of several lines from her important work, *The Watchman's Rattle: Thinking Our Way Out of Extinction* (Vanguard Press 2010).

No part of this book may be reproduced or transmitted in any form or by any means, electronic or mechanical, including photocopying, recording, or by any information storage and retrieval system, without permission in writing from the publisher. For more, please visit SetonPublishing.com.

ISBN-13: 978-0-9989605-7-9

ISBN-10: 0-9989605-7-8

Printed in the United States of America

Author's Note

When I mentioned to friends that I was writing a novel about how public education might be reformed, the immediate response was something of a pshaw nature. Why a novel, they asked? I winced and noted that people like to be entertained as well as informed, and there's enough unentertaining information out there already. Too much, it seems. So just as they are more likely to gravitate to a feature film than to a documentary, so I've written my case for school reform in a work of fiction.

When I elucidated some of the concepts I was touting, through the characters in this book, my friends' dismissive responses were dramatically mitigated by their interest and agreement. Even enthusiasm.

They wondered where the funding for the reforms I was describing would come from and I told them the primary seed funding would be coming from private sources. Uh-huh. But when I noted that parents would be more than willing to pick up the tab for their bright children getting excellent educations, there was yes-nodding all around.

In truth, the hunger for a quality school system and a reversal of the catastrophic dumbing down of America – and much of the developed world – has quickly opened the minds of instinctive skeptics to the possibility that there are solutions.

The Bright Wise Solution

So yes, this is a novel, the characters aren't real, and *The New York Tribune* hasn't been published since 1866. But the changes to our public schools suggested in these pages are hardly beyond the pale. Details would have to be worked out, but if a test market of these ideas could be established – and these concepts demonstrated their likely success – then we could certainly have a viable path to follow. It might not be straight, but at least there would be promise and hope.

Tony Seton
June 2018

Epigraph

In Sir Arthur Conan Doyle's *The Naval Treaty*, Sherlock Holmes and Dr. Watson were riding on a train out of London toward Portsmouth, and Holmes remarked, "It's a very cheering thing to come into London by any of these lines which run high and allow you to look down upon the houses like this. Look at those big, isolated clumps of buildings rising up above the slates, like brick islands in a lead-coloured sea."

"The Board Schools," replied Watson.

"Lighthouses, my boy! Beacons of the future! Capsules, with hundreds of bright little seeds in each, out of which will spring the wiser, better England of the future."

The Bright Wise Solution

Introduction

Allyson Whyte used to be teased throughout her school years for her name because she was brown. A beautiful brown girl, the daughter of a white OBGYN father from a Boston Brahman family and a dark Dartmouth political science professor born in the slums of Kingston, Jamaica. Now 45, Allyson was a beautiful woman, slightly weathered from more than two decades as an international correspondent for the *New York Tribune.*

Allyson, too, had married a white man, Wallace Priest, a news producer for CNN. They had come together during the horrific fighting in Bosnia-Herzegovina, and while linked up in their feelings for each other, were not ready in their early twenties to compromise their career plans. It was very convenient, though, that they were both based at their companies' Boston bureaus.

Putting some pressure on those plans some five years into the relationship was the arrival of their son, a healthy child who in his early years always enjoyed the quality attention of at least one or the other of his parents. It was an arrangement invoked by two very caring adults who not only loved young Michael deeply, but also thought of him as the future. Sometimes his parents' best intentions were cast asunder, as happens in the news business, but four dedicated grandparents were always ready to step in to make sure that Michael had the loving presence and intelligent caring to further – indeed enhance – his maturing into a bright and conscious young man.

There had been serious discussions among all the adults about his upbringing and particularly his schooling, but all six adults were clear that while the boy needed exposure to different cultures, that did not mean he had to attend the incessantly deteriorating public schools. The grandparents were glad to foot the considerable bills to make sure that Michael got the finest private school education available, starting in kindergarten day school and now carrying through his high school years. Note too, that his forebears also "spent" much of their free time talking and reading to the child, starting before he was even born. And of course, there was virtually no television for the boy.

To the family's pride but not surprise, Michael had scored in the top one percentile on his SSATs, and he had aced his interview with the admissions dean to gain early acceptance to Phillips Exeter Academy. There were also letters from alums who knew both the family and the boy supporting his application. Yes, everyone knew that his ethnicity was a plus since the crippled public school system was not producing many bright colored students, but they also knew that Michael's human qualities would likely open those who met him to a higher level of acceptance of other non-whites.

Now in the summer before his last year at Exeter, Michael was signed up for a tutoring project in the Roxbury section of Boston. He would be helping other teens to better read, write, and speak English so that they might advance themselves to higher education and better jobs.

The Bright Wise Solution

The broader purpose of the program was to engage young people to improve the quality of life for themselves and succeeding generations.

The Bright Wise Solution

Chapter One

Allyson Whyte arrived at the gate for her flight just as the last call for boarding was being made. She walked up to the counter with her ticket and pre-printed boarding card and handed them to the woman at the counter.

The woman frowned, checked her computer screen, and sighed, anticipating a fight. "I'm sorry, Miz" – she looked again at the ticket – "Whyte. The flight is full. There are no seats left."

Allyson deliberately pushed out of her mind the possibility that she was being dealt with differently, especially being in the south. She didn't want that to feed her annoyance that could move her to anger. Allyson said distinctly, "What do you mean it's full? I have a ticket. I have a boarding pass. And I have to get back to Boston, now."

The woman had heard this all before. "I'm sorry, the plane is full. I can see about putting you on the next flight." She typed on her keyboard.

A manager had been observing this from the background. He stepped forward and picked up the ticket and boarding pass, looking at them closely. Then he spoke quietly to the counter agent, who responded by typing on her keyboard. Then she looked up from the screen to her manager.

He nodded briefly to the agent and addressed the customer. "Excuse me, but aren't you the Allyson Whyte, the reporter for the *New York Tribune*?"

Allyson was clearly surprised at being recognized, but she was also wary. "Yes. Yes I am."

"Ms. Whyte, your pieces on Parkland have been first rate. I am looking forward to how you covered today's memorial service."

A smile broke over Allyson's face. "Why thank you. That's very nice."

He looked down at the computer screen, confirming, and gave direction to the counter woman. Then he spoke to Allyson. "I'm sorry about this mix up. We were overwhelmed by the number of people leaving Miami today. I wonder if it would be all right if we offered you a seat in the front cabin. At no extra charge, of course."

"Thank you, Mr." – she read his name tag – "Mr. Lopez, but I'm afraid it's against company policy to accept gifts."

"Oh, this isn't a gift, Ms. Whyte. It is resolving our over-booking error."

Allyson smiled. "Well then, yes, thank you. I'd be delighted to accept your resolution of your over-booking error."

Mr. Lopez smiled back and looked over his shoulder at the gate door, checking to see if the person who was getting bumped off the flight to make room for her was out yet. He conferred again with the counter agent. After another minute, he looked down the gangway again, and turning back, there was a frown on his face. He switched to a smile, and said to Allyson, "I'll just be a minute." He walked down the gangway and in less than a minute a man in a suit carrying an airline briefcase was walking up the gangway. He spied Allyson at the counter and gave her something of a muted glare before leaving the gate area. Mr. Lopez was only a few seconds behind the man. He came for Allyson and took her to her seat on the plane.

"Thank you, Mr. Lopez. I really appreciate this extra courtesy. It was important for me to be back in Boston tonight."

"Of course, Ms. Whyte. Thank you for your patience. Have a good flight." With that he turned and left the aircraft. No sooner had he gone than the door was closed and the flight attendants made ready for departure.

Allyson slipped her carry-on below the seat in front of her, sat down and belted up. It was then she could take a deep breath and check out her surroundings. While boarding she had observed that the first class cabin was full but for one aisle seat in the middle of the section. She had noticed the looks of interest that she had gotten from one of the flight attendants; curiosity, she decided rather than opprobrium. Then Allyson turned to greet her seat mate.

"Hi, Allyson Whyte," she said to the tall man, probably in his sixties, she decided, noting also that he was upscale, casual, neat, healthy, and white. "I hope I didn't hold you up."

He smiled back at her. "I'm not in a hurry." He offered his hand. "Laurence Selden. Pleased to meet you, Ms. Whyte. I trust we're both headed to Boston?"

She laughed, "I certainly hope so. Is that where you live?"

"I've spent a lot of time in the area, but no, I live in the western part of the state. Stockbridge."

"Oh that's a lovely spot. You've got a bit of a drive to get home."

"A couple of hours, but I have a friend who's doing the driving. Do you live in town?"

"No, about a half-hour out, in Westwood."

"That's a nice area, too." He asked her, "Were you in Miami for Parkland?"

Allyson peered at him. "Actually I was." Then she added, "but not related to anyone."

Laurence raised his eyebrows, asking.

"I'm a journalist. I was covering the memorial service today."

"That must have been a challenge. So much pain, so much frustration about nothing being done."

"It was palpable," she concurred, her tone of voice raising the gradient a level.

The plane had taxied onto the runway and was beginning to roll. The two sat back in their seats. When the plane had climbed to 10,000 feet, they resumed their conversation.

"Were you in Miami on business?" Allyson asked.

"I was, over in Naples, actually, on the other side of the state."

Allyson waited.

"I consult school systems on how to improve the engagement of their students."

"And how can they do that?"

"First they have to know how important it is. It's news to some teachers and administrators, but when they find the students more attentive, when they are getting questions back from the students that show they want to know more, the teachers are quickly and enthusiastically on board."

"That must be very rewarding for everyone concerned, at the schools and for yourself. I'd be very interested in learning more about how you are accomplishing this. What you are doing."

"Would you?" He chuckled and shook his head. "You know, most people haven't the slightest interest in my work."

"Oh my goodness, if you are successful in what you do – you are, I presume, aren't you?" – he smiled and nodded – "Then what you're doing should be shared widely."

He looked at her closely. "And might you, as a journalist, be able to do that?"

She smiled back. "Yes, and with people who would immediately appreciate how important this is."

Chapter Two

The plane landed at Logan Airport on time, and Laurence and Allyson were making their way through the terminal. They stopped together at the baggage claim area where Allyson was to wait for her bag. With only his carry-on bag, Laurence was ready to connect with his driver for the ride to Stockbridge.

"You have my card, Allyson. I look forward to hearing from you."

"Thank you, Laurence, and I promise it will be soon. I know the editors will want me to pursue this with you."

They shook hands and he departed. Allyson opened up her cellphone and speed-dialed a number. She waited only a moment and the call was answered.

"Hi, mom," she said in a happy, glad-to-be-home voice. "We just got in. I'm waiting for my bag."

Standing in the kitchen of Allyson's home, Clarice Whyte replied, "Hi honey, welcome home. Looking forward to seeing you."

Allyson heard something in her voice. "What is it, Mom? Is everything all right?"

"It is now, hon. There was a minor kerfuffle after Michael's tutoring session this afternoon."

The Bright Wise Solution

"What happened?" Allyson demanded, trying not to panic.

"He's all right, Ally," her mother insisted in a forced soothing tone. "A mother was unhappy with something he had said to his students, and she hit him with her pocketbook. He got a little scratch. Nothing serious. He's fine."

Allyson was quiet but seething. It was not all right. "You're sure *my son* is fine."

Clarice fought down her inclination to be defensive. "Allyson, Michael is all right. He received little more than a scratch. And, I might add, he behaved himself as the perfect gentleman you have brought him up to be." She silently mouthed, "We have brought him up to be."

Allyson heard herself. "Okay. Sorry. I'll be home within the hour."

* * * * *

Allyson pulled into the two-car driveway of her nicely-appointed two-story home in the upper middle-class neighborhood where she and her husband had lived since shortly after they had met. She grabbed her bags and went into the house by way of the kitchen door. The warmth of the room and the smells of food cooking helped to improve her mood.

Clarice, her mother, a very alive 70, walked into the kitchen from the dining room where she was setting the table for dinner for three. Allyson had just put down her bags. She stepped away from them and gave her mother a hug. Disengaged, she looked around, obviously disappointed that Michael wasn't there to greet her.

Seeing her daughter's expression, her mother said extra

warmly, "Hi, honey. Glad you're home."

"Where's Michael?"

"He's over at Ronnie's shooting hoops. I'm sure he'll be home in a couple of minutes. You made good time from the airport."

Allyson nodded her acknowledgment. "So what happened?"

"To Michael?" her mother asked innocently.

Allyson had to laugh. "All right, he's fine. I just don't like anyone hurting my boy."

"No, and *your* mother doesn't like her grandson being hit by someone. But now you know he's all right, so I'll let him tell you what happened." She added, "And then we can talk about what to do about it."

That got her daughter's attention. There was the sound of a basketball being bounced in the driveway, heading their way. In a moment, the bouncing stopped, the door opened, and in walked Michael, a tall, athletic 17-year-old with a happy expression on his bright face, somewhat marred by a bandage on his left cheek.

"Hi, Mom," he said, a slight tentativeness in his voice, knowing her concern. He gave her a big hug.

"Let me see," she told him, pulling out of the hug but holding her son near.

He faced her directly and when she bent her head to look more closely at his cheek, teasingly he tilted his head away so it was harder to see.

"Hey, let me see."

"Come on, Mom. It's nothing. Just a scratch. Anyway

you can't see under the bandage."

"Did it bleed a lot?"

"No."

"Does it hurt?"

"No, Mom, it really wasn't a big deal."

Allyson relented, and guiding her son to a seat at the kitchen table and taking one herself, she ordered, "Tell me what happened."

Michael took a deep breath and let it out. "Well, I'd finished the class and walked out of the school, and there was Mrs. Southern standing there."

"She was waiting for you?"

He thought a moment and then said, "Yeah. Yes," he corrected.

"And?"

"And so I walked toward the gate and was gonna go around her but she said, 'What ya saying to mah baby?' She talks like that. Anyway, she meant her 14-year-old son whom I'm tutoring in English."

"And I told her, 'I'm teaching him English.'"

"'He don't need to know no English. He already speaks it...good.'"

"I shrugged my shoulders. I didn't want to argue with her."

Clarice interjected, "Smart boy."

Allyson didn't take her eyes off her son.

"She said, 'You tole him he's not African-American.'"

"Uh-oh," said Allyson.

"No, Mom, I was just saying in class what you and dad, grandma and grandpa say, that you don't want to put African in front of American, because we're Americans, and hyphenating it is divisive."

"And what did she say to that?"

Michael looked down and winced, then looked back up at his mother. "She didn't give me time to say that, to explain, she just called me a 'damn Oreo' and hit me with her bag and left."

"Oh, Michael, my dear boy, I'm so sorry." She looked with pride and anguish at her son. "Who bandaged your face?"

He shrugged. "I went into the school to the administration office and the nurse took care of it. She wiped it clean, put some Neosporin on it, and the bandage."

"And did you report what happened to anyone?"

"No, the nurse asked, and I told her, and she must have told Miss Harmony, who's running the summer tutoring program. Then when I was leaving, Miss Harmony, came out and asked me to tell her what happened. And I did."

"What did she say?"

"Nothing, just not to tell anyone about it. That we – she said 'we' – we don't want to make waves and disturb the community."

Allyson sat back in her chair and sighed. "I suppose I understand her point of view," she said resignedly.

There was silence, and then in a commanding voice her mother declared, "Understand, maybe, but that's not all right. That woman assaulted a person, a teacher for goodness' sake, and not for doing anything bad or even wrong."

Allyson said to them, "We don't have to blow this out of proportion…"

"Yes *we* do. Not out of proportion, but we can't let them roll over Michael. If you don't want to do what's right – what needs to be done – then I will. It's not all right for people to go around assaulting teachers – especially a 17-year-old – a brilliant, good, young man, who's not getting paid, volunteering his time and attention and intelligence to help people climb out of ignorance and poverty – no ma'am!"

Allyson and Michael were startled at her vehemence.

"I am fed up with this nonsense of the school administrators thinking that their teachers are there to be punching bags for ignorant parents and students who think they can take out their frustrations on people who are trying to make this a better world.

"Honey," Clarice said in an appreciably calmer tone, "I know you have to go to work, but I'm not due back at Dartmouth for another week. I'm going to the police tomorrow and file assault charges against that woman, and I'm bringing Michael with me, not only to show-'n-tell what happened, but also for him to learn what it means to stand up against evil." She sat down at the table across from them.

There was a long silence, and then Allyson reached out a hand to each of them; Clarice and Michael also joined hands. Allyson spoke. "You're right, Mom. Being nice, taking it because we have some sort of mixed up sense of guilt about having an education…it's not working."

"It never could," put in her mother gently but still firmly.

"No, you're right." Allyson took a deep breath and let it out. "I would be most grateful if you would take Michael into the city tomorrow and file a complaint with the police." She turned to her son. "How would you feel about being done with the tutoring? I know there are six weeks left, but I don't want to have to worry about you. What might happen when this angry mother is charged with assault. How her friends or relatives might react."

Michael leaned over and put his head on his mother's shoulder. "That would be fine with me, Mom. Grandma is right about the schools not protecting us. All they care about is getting funding, which they do by filling seats, not whether the kids learn anything. Besides, most of them in my class aren't paying attention. They're either on their phones or sleeping."

"You're kidding?" demanded his mother, surprised.

"No," he said after a moment, "not at all. And with some of them, I'm glad that's all they're doing."

"Then you're done," his mother said, anger and decision clarion in her voice.

Chapter Three

The next morning Allyson was in her office in Boston where she held the title of the *Tribune's* New England Bureau Chief. She was listening on the speakerphone to the morning editorial meeting connecting the seven domestic bureau chiefs. Allyson had pushed the mute button to reduce the amount of ambient noise of conversations, ringing phones, and traffic noise coming from outside her office. Conducting the meeting from his office in New York was the domestic news editor, Jeff Platen.

"So I guess that's it for the moment. We'll meet here again at three to see how the world has turned, or at least our part of it. Ally, don't go anywhere. I need to talk to you. I'll call you in fifteen."

She started to reply and then remembered to push the mute off. "Right, Jeff. I'll be here," she said, and then clicked off the call. She walked out into the newsroom and made herself a cup of Kona decaf, sipping it slowly as she looked out of their fifth-floor picture window at the city that stretched out to the northeast, where she could see in the not too great distance jets flying in and out of Logan Airport. She returned to her office, sat down at her desk, and was writing up her expense account when her phone rang.

"Hi, Jeff."

"Hey, hon, good job on Parkland. Kudos from upstairs."

Allyson smiled. She was always comforted when the big bosses bothered to pass along praise for a story to come out of her bureau. "Funny," she thought, "when it's about me, it's not as important, because the people upstairs are more the executive types than the serious journalists." Still, she was glad to hear, too, that they liked her work.

"Thanks. A hard story to mess up."

"Pshaw, you humble thing you. You know how to blend the facts with the emotions, to communicate the feelings without sounding maudlin. Good stuff."

"Thanks, Jeff."

Platen was a serious journalist, despite his managerial position, so his praise – and his increasingly infrequent criticism – were greatly valued by her.

"Anyway, upstairs likes the writing that's coming out of your neighborhood, and wants to get some enterprise reporting from you and your folks. When you don't have anything breaking, of course."

"That's great. For the magazine?"

"Um, no, actually. They are going to put more feature stories on the front page. Like what the *Washington Post* is doing, and some other papers. And doing some more videos."

"'Hmm', she said."

"Yeah, I'm not sure it's such a good idea either, squeezing out the hard news so to attract readers, but I don't make those decisions."

The Bright Wise Solution

"Hmm again. But okay."

"Anything you think you want to look at, Ally?"

She thought but a moment and replied, "Actually there is. I met an interesting fellow on the flight up from Miami yesterday. He's a school consultant who is focused on engaging the students. He particularly shows teachers how to make the classes relevant to the students' lives, and it seems to be working." She paused. "And it's not working in many places around the country, not just the poorer parts of the cities. The teachers have their hands tied by all sorts of rules, and the school administrators continue to make matters worse."

"That's what the right-wingers are saying about Parkland, isn't it?"

"That was partially the problem, yes. Social politics. People claiming race is the issue instead of confronting what's really upsetting things. Teachers burned out or on drugs. Funding issues. Students who don't know why they are there."

There was silence on the other end of the phone. She continued, "I know it's huge, Jeff, and we could report new aspects of it seven days a week, but there are some key points that might produce some important reporting, and maybe generate some advertising..."

"...And win us some recognition. I like it, Ally. And I want to give you some help."

"Help?"

"Yeah, I got this kid, well, he's 30-ish, who started as copy boy at ABC a while back and worked his way up. He's been in the biz for a dozen years, mostly online, places like *The Intercept* and *TruthOut*. But he's not far left in his thinking. Progressive, but grounded."

"Sounds like us when we were young."

"Gimme a break. You're hardly an antique, Ally."

"Okay, when you were young."

They laughed together. "So I'm gonna send him up to you for the next month or so, give him some seasoning. You can see if you think he has promise."

"What's his job title?"

"Cub reporter?" he joked. "I don't know. He'll be on my budget, but he's working for you. Use him yourself, maybe on this education story, or have him work with your other people. Probably keep him in-house for the first month...or not. You know what you're doing."

"That sounds good, Jeff. Thanks. What's his name and when should I expect him? And I trust he's not sleeping on the couch in the lobby?"

"His name is Drew Ekland. He has relatives in Cambridge who are putting him up, and he should be arriving this afternoon, probably in the office tomorrow. I recall you have an extra desk in the newsroom, yes?"

"We'll be fine, yes. I trust you gave him my cell if he needs another way of communicating."

"Of course. But Ally, I think you will find this 'kid' older than his years."

"The Fourth Estate could certainly benefit from some new grown-ups. Thanks again, Jeff. One of us will call you when he's arrived."

Chapter Four

Clarice and Michael drove into Boston to the police station whose jurisdiction included the school yard where the assault took place. When they arrived, parking in the police lot, they went inside and Clarice spoke to the desk sergeant about filing an assault charge on behalf of her grandson, pointing to the bandage on his face.

The sergeant, an older man, or at least he looked older than he was by years, had a round, red face and white hair. He looked them both over carefully and with a thoughtful look on his face, he picked up the phone on his desk and held a brief conversation with someone on the other end. When he hung up, he told them someone would be right out for them.

And it was less than a minute that a black woman in a lieutenant's uniform came out into the lobby, and introduced herself as Lt. Laurie Raimonde. She brought them back to her office. After the three were seated, she said she was told that they wanted to file an assault charge.

"Could you tell me what happened, please?" she asked directing her question to the grandmother.

Clarice responded, "This is my grandson, Michael Whyte. What happened happened to him. He's remarkably articulate. I would like him to tell you why we are here."

"Of course," said the lieutenant who nodded at Michael.

Michael told the lieutenant exactly and concisely what had happened in full detail, through to the advice from Miss Harmony, the tutoring program administrator, that he not to tell what had occurred.

The lieutenant thought for a long moment and then, looking at the both of them, said, "Are you sure you want to go through with filing this complaint? You were not badly injured."

Clarice looked at Michael who answered, "I had questions about it but my grandma is right."

"What do you mean?" the lieutenant asked.

"Well, we have a tendency to let people go, particularly those who are at the lower end of the economic ladder because we feel guilty because we are doing better than they are. But it's not okay to hit someone. Violence is not the answer."

A small smile widened slowly on the lieutenant's face. She said to Michael, "I'm sure you would rather have let this go away, but I'm really honored that you are here to speak your mind. Because you are right. We do too often give away what's right because of our guilt. Yes, we will take care of this for you. I just need some details."

Michael filled in the blanks with the times and people he'd dealt with, the correct spelling of their names, titles, and contact information. When he was finished and Lieutenant Raimonde had rechecked her notes, she said, "Good. I have what I need."

The two then stood to leave and moved to the door. But

The Bright Wise Solution

then Clarice stopped and turned and said, "I hope you don't mind my asking, but your desk sergeant seemed to give some thought about whom we should speak to. I don't know if he would normally have handled it himself, but obviously he chose the right person. I was wondering..." she shrugged her shoulders.

The lieutenant, standing behind her desk, nodded and smiled. "Sergeant Rose," she explained, "is a very good man. Old Irish stock. A police veteran, I think he's been here 29 years. And we've been having an ongoing conversation about how difficult it is for blacks to climb up in our society. He said he thought it became particularly harder when the cops tried to give them a break because they lacked education or money or character. In fact, it made them feel worse because they saw themselves as treated differently because they weren't as good as other people."

"Oh, my goodness," Michael said involuntarily, earning respectful looks from his grandmother and the lieutenant.

The lieutenant observed to the young man, "Privilege is not a bad thing in and of itself, Michael, especially if you've earned it. But even if you inherited it, even more especially, if you do something with that privilege to make this a better world."

Clarice nodded and said, "Yes, ma'am..." And then amended, "...Lieutenant. And thank you."

They left her office and as they were going through the lobby, Clarice stopped in front of the desk sergeant and touched Michael's shoulder. Michael looked up at her and saw her looking at the policeman.

"Thank you, Sergeant," Michael said, "for your service."

The sergeant was briefly flustered. "Why thank you, and for your being a good citizen."

They nodded to each other, and then his very proud grandmother led her grandson out of the police station.

Chapter Five

Her mother was sitting at the kitchen table when Allyson got home. Clarice told her daughter about their experience at the police station. Both women expressed their pride for what Michael had done. The boy had been standing at the kitchen counter making himself a sandwich, his face turned away, smiling and occasionally raising his eyebrows at what he'd heard.

"The lieutenant certainly nailed it, didn't she?" Allyson asked rhetorically. "And it's ironic that she, and we, and so many of our black friends, also feel the guilt of education and financial stability."

"Doesn't it underscore that it isn't about the color of a person's skin," her mother said, "but her ability to manage life. You know the circumstances of your grandparents in the slums of Kingston. How hard they worked to get us out and to America. And not just labor, but their spirit. They never stopped trying new ways to help us to escape that life of poverty and violence."

"Why is it, do you suppose, that people don't make that effort?" Allyson asked her mother. "I would think that it is basic human instinct to rise above where they are."

"It probably is instinctual, but a hard life can pull the plug on them." Clarice thought for a moment. "But when you have people around you nurturing you, pushing you to succeed, then that light should grow into something greater. As with our dear Michael."

Allyson pulled out her phone and tapped some keys for a search. She quickly found what she was looking for. "You reminded me of a wonderful quote from George Bernard Shaw. 'This is the true joy of life, the being used for a purpose recognized by yourself as a mighty one, the being a force of nature instead of a feverish, selfish little clod of ailments and grievances, complaining that the world will not devote itself to making you happy. I am of the opinion that my life belongs to the whole community, and as long as I live, it is my privilege to do for it whatever I can. I want to be thoroughly used up when I die, for the harder I work, the more I live. I rejoice in life for its own sake. Life is no 'brief candle' to me. It is a sort of splendid torch which I got hold of for the moment, and I want to make it burn as brightly as possible before handing it on to further generations.' I think that's a marvelous perspective."

"Yes, it is right," her mother agreed. "Don't you think, Michael?"

"Yes, Grandma," he said showing considerable patience in his tone. He picked up his plate and glass and started to walk away but stopped by the table when his mother spoke to him.

"I'm very proud of you, Michael, for the way you handled yourself today. I know your father will be, too, when I tell him later."

Michael's eyebrows went up though there was an obvious smile in his mind. "Mom, this is sort of what the lieutenant said. Except maybe the converse. You are praising me for what I should do. Isn't that kind of the same thing as letting people go because we feel guilty about being privileged?"

Allyson looked at Clarice and in a moment they both broke out in laughter. "Yes, Michael, to make up for it, I should send you up to bed without dinner. And no watching television."

"I don't have a television, Mom, but you better let me have dinner or I'll call that lieutenant and tell her you're abusing me."

The adults laughed again as Michael turned to hide his own pleased expression and left the room.

Chapter Six

The next morning found Allyson driving west on the Massachusetts Turnpike. Next to her was Drew Ekland, the new addition to her staff who had arrived at the bureau the afternoon before. He'd only spent a short time getting acclimated to his new office situation before he headed off with his luggage to park himself in his new digs.

"I thought this would be a productive way to get to know each other," she explained.

"No interruptions," he agreed.

"So four questions for you, Drew. Who are you, how did you get here, where do you want to go, and what is your route?"

He chuckled. "That should wrap things up. Okay, I'm a journalist, proud to be a laborer in the Fourth Estate vineyard. I started writing for the local newspaper when I was 13, covering the junior high sports teams. This was in Palo Alto. We'd moved there when I was seven. I was editor of the school paper there in my senior year. I went to Oberlin, where there wasn't much media, so I focused on American history and English. We did a lot of writing in different formats.

"It wasn't what I really cared for, but I told myself I was

expanding my horizons." He looked over at Allyson who couldn't help but smile. "Then in the spring of my sophomore year, I was on Easter break visiting with my Uncle Stanley and Aunt Adele in New York. I was always closer to him than to my father, and we had a long talk about what I wanted to be when I grew up. I was clear then about journalism, and my uncle arranged for me to have lunch with a friend of his who was a radio time buyer." His mind searched. "Nick Madona was his name. He got me an interview for a desk assistant's position – that's a low-pay copy boy – at ABC network, and ten days later I was offered a job.

"My father said I should first finish my four years of college and get a diploma. Uncle Stanley wondered if I needed that diploma. He said, 'It's not like you're avoiding the draft like we were during the Vietnam War.' I agreed with my uncle. And ABC was very nice. They let me finish the semester, and I started there in late May ten years ago."

"That must have been a thrill for you...living in New York, working for the network."

He gave her a big smile, pleased that she understood so easily. "It was great. I so knew where I was and what I wanted to do.

"I stayed there for four years, moving up the ladder first as a newswriter and then as an assistant and later an associate producer. I did some traveling with them, too. It was quite exciting."

"But?"

"But it was always on deadline. Not that I think we should stop the presses, but too often I felt coverage was cut off of a story that needed more consideration."

Allyson nodded.

"I also thought that the networks – all of them, except for Fox and MSNBC which were blowing their own smoke – were all doing he said-she said reporting, and that was shortchanging the story. I mean, wasn't it Edward R. Murrow who said there aren't always two sides to every story?"

"Yes, and a favorite quote of mine."

"So I went to work for *The Intercept* because I respected the people who set it up, and then I did a stint at *Truth-Out*."

"And why did you leave there?"

"Because I wanted to get back to journalism with a broader audience. Those last two gigs were more preaching to the choir."

"Uh-huh."

Drew sighed. "As far as where do I want to go and how am I going to get there...dunno. I think of the line in one of Vonnegut's short stories about life being 'one foot in front of the other, through leaves, over bridges.' I'm comfortable with not knowing."

"Good for you. An open mind about your future clearly reflects an openness toward what's happening in the world, what you're covering as a journalist. Fewer misconceptions and biases about what you're investigating."

"I hadn't thought about it that way, but you're right. I like that. Thank you," he added.

They drove in silence for a while and then Drew asked, "What about you? How did you get to where you are? Oh, and how is it that the New England bureau chief was

The Bright Wise Solution

covering Parkland?"

"I started with the *AP* as a stringer when I was at Radcliffe, and after being in the right place at the right time on a couple of stories, I was offered a reporting job at the *Tribune*. That was almost 20 years ago. As far as Parkland was concerned, I was speaking at a conference on civil rights in Boca Raton when the shooting started. I was closer than our people in Miami, so I covered it from the start. That's why they sent me back last week to cover up to and through the memorial service."

They drove in silence for a few minutes, and Drew asked, "What do you want from me? Is that why we're going to meet this fellow in Stockbridge?"

"I told you yesterday about my conversation with Jeff Platen and my interest in looking into what's wrong with our public schools. Laurence is a very bright fellow who knows what's wrong with them and what must be done to make them work. I want you to absorb what he says and develop a relationship with him so that you can get whatever information we might need on the subject." She took a quick glance at the young man. "And so you know, I expect that you will be doing more than research. There will be some travel and a role in the reporting. From what I know about you – from what you've told me and from Jeff, and my own digging – I thought this might be an interesting adventure for you."

* * * * *

"I didn't realize how bad things were," Drew said as they were driving back to Boston several hours later. "It's upending the very foundation of our country. Democracy can't survive if the people aren't informed, aren't engaged."

"You can see why I wanted you to meet Laurence."

"Oh certainly. He really knows his stuff. How providential that you sat next to him on the plane."

Allyson pondered the comment for a moment and agreed. "Yes...Providential."

Chapter Seven

"Not everything is providential," Allyson commented obliquely to her mother. They were sitting in the kitchen.

Clarice was filling her daughter in on the day's news from the home front. "Because we filed the complaint with the police against the Southern woman for assault, the school fired Michael and sent a letter to Exeter saying that Michael was fired for refusing to follow instructions, and that he would not be invited back to participate in their program."

"Oh goodness, how can they be so awful? The woman hit him. He didn't do anything wrong. What's wrong with them?"

"Now not to worry, Allyson," her mother commanded. "I've got this under control."

Her daughter shot her a skeptical look.

"Really I have. I called a friend of mine, Anthony Bonifaccio— "

"The conservative lawyer?" Allyson asked, alarmed.

"Honey, he's more progressive than a lot of liberals, and he's got a great record of bringing down government agencies that have lost sight of their mission."

The expression on her face said that Allyson had to be

convinced.

"You remember how Anthony went after the human rights director in the Chicago DA's office who said blacks deserved to go to the head of the line for alternative justice programs?"

Allyson nodded her head slowly. "Yes, I remember."

"And you remember how he was castigated by the left?"

Allyson nodded again. "So what does he say about Michael's situation?"

Clarice sat back in her chair and smiled. "He's furious and delighted. This is just the sort of situation he wants to straighten out."

"And?"

"And he's looking at a lawsuit against the school principal and the school district for accessory to assault and battery, and defamation of character."

"Good lord!"

"And he's confident they'll wind up settling."

"How much will he cost?"

"Us? Not a penny. He might take something out of the settlement." A smile grew on her mother's face. "It gets better. First, he expects them to reluctantly agree to settle, but then they'll insist on a non-disclosure agreement."

"Hardly a surprise."

"Of course, but," she added in a triumphant voice, "Anthony will refuse. He said he'd say he wouldn't accept that condition even if they agreed to pay three times the settlement." Clarice chuckled. "Not that their insurance would have covered the higher amount to protect their clients' image. They don't mind the school getting some bad press if it's going to cost them less money. Hah!"

"Oh, Mom, I hate this. Lawyers bring out the worst in people. I don't want Michael to have anything to do with this."

"Now you listen to me, dear daughter of mine, this is about justice. It's not about lawyers and money, it's about doing the right thing. It's about slapping the wrists of some people who behaved badly, and forcing them to admit it. They will also be required to send a *mea culpa* letter on Michael's behalf to Exeter totally exonerating him and apologizing for their mishandling of the matter."

Allyson slowly relented.

Then Clarice nailed the case shut. "And of course he wants it to go public, like with the Chicago matter, to warn foolish administrators from putting their confused notions of diversity ahead of what is right. So other people, here and elsewhere, can do their jobs without being afraid of being mistreated by some foolish administrators."

Allyson sat for a moment, shaking her head at the irony of the situation. "Did you ever think we'd be on this side of this sort of situation?"

Clarice looked at her daughter, appreciating her openness to come around the way she had. "The pendulum has swung too far. It's not about left versus right. It's about wrong and right, and we must always be on the side of right."

Chapter Eight

The next morning, Drew was standing in the doorway of her office, talking to Allyson who was sitting at her desk. "I just wanted to stop by and thank you for bringing me into this schools mess."

She laughed at the reference, letting out her own feelings about the mess. "Remind me to tell you later about another angle."

He raised his eyebrows with anticipation, but she would tell him later. "Also, I was on the phone with my parents last night, telling them about my new position – not about my assignment – and how good it felt to be here. And I suddenly recalled something that I was surprised I didn't remember yesterday. When I was thirteen, we were living in Aurora, just east of Denver. I was in the eighth grade in a middle school there. And there was an incident with a teacher trying to control some children who were bussed to our school from the Latino neighborhoods in the city.

"I'm a little foggy on the details, but one day I forgot something and went back into the classroom and one of those kids had the teacher backed into a corner and she was screaming 'Get off of me.' And the kid wasn't. So I said something like, 'Hey, what are you doing? Stop that.' The kid turned around and looked at me, and when he did, the teacher gave him a shove and slipped around him and went flying out the door behind me."

"Oh my god. What happened?"

"The next day, the principal came in and introduced us to our new teacher. He didn't say what happened to Mrs. Wheeler. But he told us that we had to be patient with the children who came from other schools.

"That's what the schools' attitude is. That teachers have to accept that children will act out, and violently. I read this morning that there were over 200,000 student assaults on teachers two years ago, and that was just the number reported. It's estimated to be twice that."

"Good grief. No wonder so many teachers are on drugs or quitting the profession."

"There's a growing shortage of teachers because there is such a high burn-out rate. In California they are offering $10,000 sign-up bonuses and may waive the normal requirement for a teaching certificate."

Allyson was startled. "I knew it was bad, but not like this. Especially the violence against teachers. Drew, we need statistics and we need stories. All verified. Also, find out where the biggest problems are and why. Are we talking gangs, money, race, single parents? And we need to find out how the teachers and the unions, are reacting, and how the school districts are responding."

Drew had been writing in his notebook, and when he finished he looked up at Allyson and smiled. "The game is a-foot," he said. Then he turned and walked away.

Allyson's smile morphed into determination. "Yes," she said to herself, "Mom is right. We need to fix what's wrong right."

Chapter Nine

Allyson Whyte was on the phone with Jeff Platen.

"You nailed it, Ally," he said. "Upstairs is high-fiving each other over Drew's essay on violence against teachers."

"Drew's the one who deserves the credit, Jeff. He did an excellent job. He needed very little oversight from me, I'm pleased to say."

"Yes, of course, but don't shirk all the responsibility. It was your idea, and the folks who sign our checks are very pleased. It's amazing how the school authorities and the unions were so passive about the problem. Our readers were outraged but there was little to no response from the education officials. Upstairs is talking about the *Tribune* embracing the education issue. Making it ours.

Allyson chuckled loudly enough to be heard. "That's a good thing. We're loaded for bear."

"Whatcha got?"

"It's a situation Drew heard about from someone he talked to at the Department of Education in Washington. They've been looking at the discipline numbers going back ten years and they have found that children of color are being disciplined two or three times more often than whites."

The Bright Wise Solution

"I can't stand that term, 'of color.' It's like white isn't a color. It's so divisive."

There was silence on Allyson's end. "That's part of the problem, and part of the story."

"Go ahead. Sorry. I'll try not to interrupt but you know I can't help it."

She chuckled again. "The Ed secretary is threatening to withhold federal funding to schools with disproportionate long-term suspension, expulsion, and other severe discipline rates that seem to indicate a bias."

"But is it racism, Ally, or are these kids just behaving worse? I mean, they come from poor neighborhoods, no fathers, drugs, violence, right?"

Allyson smiled at the interruption. "You've put your finger on the crux of the problem, Jeff. No one seems to be acknowledging that aspect. Are they being disciplined because of color or because of behavior?"

"That's crazy," her editor said, clearly riled. "But why?"

Allyson let out a deep breath. "It is crazy. My take is that it's liberal guilt, misplaced and over the top. I used to think of myself as a liberal, but not anymore. These people aren't making sense. They're so obsessed with diversity, with multiculturalism, that they refuse to see that the misfits in the classroom – the dangerous ones, those who are unprepared to be in a classroom, those who are malnourished; the list of problems is long – are not only unable to function as students, but they are ruining the class for everyone else."

Allyson paused, and when she continued, it was in a less hurried voice. "Of course there's racism, but, Jeff, from my experience and observations over the last couple of decades, there's a lot less than there used to be. But we're talking about it more. It's on the front pages of the news almost daily. The fact is, we need to talk about it less, except the truly egregious situations, and let things quiet down. It takes generations for social ills like racism to be filtered out, or at least down."

Jeff was quiet almost long enough for Allyson to ask if he was still on the line, but then he spoke in a very measured tone. "This is very hot, Ally. Politically. It's blaming the liberals – the champions of education – for the collapse of our schools."

Allyson became the editor. "I don't think we should put it that way, Jeff. We'll lose people who know there's a crisis, but don't want it all pulled up by the roots, so to say. I would at least start with the premise about the road to hell being paved with good intentions."

"Yeah, I know. In truth, the road to hell simply leads to no good. This approach to discipline in the schools looks like a stepchild of affirmative action. Of course we want to level the playing field, but it can't be done by simply declaring that everyone is equal."

"Yes, and that's what happened in the schools in Aurora. Worse. They said the teachers had to put up with the huge cultural differences of the Latino children – like the boys dominating the girls, and a more permissive attitude toward physical force – for three years."

"That was a policy? You're kidding. That's crazier than crazy. What happened?"

"Well, that's one of the school districts that is being threatened by Washington. Drew is working on a draft now. I should see something next week and then I'll forward it to you."

"Good. What's next from you? I trust you have another piece for us."

"There is one, Jeff, and it's sort of personal. I think you should assign someone from the New York office to cover it."

"You are lighting fires up there? Tell me."

"I'll send you a synopsis in an hour."

Jeff laughed.

"What?" she asked, appreciating his tone with a smile he couldn't see.

"Oh, I was just remembering when I decided to hire you, what was it, some 20 years ago?" He paused. "I had to persuade someone to give you a try. He was leery, saying you didn't have much experience, but I pushed because I had a feeling about you." He paused again for effect. "And I certainly was right."

Chapter Ten

It was late morning in early September and in front of the school where Michael Whyte had been a tutor, Anthony Bonifaccio stood in front of a gaggle of media and some onlookers. A big man who had played defense for the Big Green football squad at Dartmouth, he had more than his size to garner attention. He was a flashy dresser, taking advantage of his olive complexion with bright but well-matched colors in his expensive appearance. Also present, at a distance, a number of adults could be seen in the windows of the school building in the background, looking out at the circus.

"I am here today," he began, "to announce a settlement with the Roxbury public school system. They have agreed to pay a substantial amount of punitive funds for their mistreatment of a young man who taught here last summer. He was a volunteer tutor who was respected by the other teachers here, most of whom won't speak on the record for fear of retribution, and he was well-liked by his students."

"Where is he, Anthony?" shouted one of the reporters. Another called out, "Why isn't he here with you today?"

The attorney didn't like to be interrupted but he took advantage of the second question. "I'm glad you asked that, Butch. Because he's a minor, and because he's humble; he doesn't want any publicity." He cleared his throat. "So I trust you will, please, respect his family's desire for privacy. They didn't choose this fight. Also, the boy is still in school and he didn't want to miss any classes."

He looked away from the particular reporter and continued. "This boy – he is really a young man – was a fine tutor. He was helping young people from this neighborhood to learn to express themselves better. It happened that one day, one of his students asked him why he didn't refer to himself as an African-American. The young man told the class that like his mother and his grandmother, he didn't believe in putting any label in front of calling himself an American."

Bonifaccio let that sit for a moment. "Smart kid. A real American. Doesn't want to be divisive. And what happens? He leaves the school one day, and he's confronted by the mother of the student who asked that question, and before he has a chance to explain, she smashes him in the face with her pocketbook, cutting him on the cheek."

Again he paused. "He went back inside the school to see the nurse who fixed him up. It wasn't a deep wound. When asked by the person running the tutorial program what had happened, the nurse told her. And this principal told the young tutor that he shouldn't say anything about the incident because it could cause a bad feeling in the community.

"Now what kind of nonsense is that? Here a young man, doing good for the neighborhood, and he's assaulted by a grown-up who lacks the basic decency to let someone explain what happened, what a bright thought he had shared with his students, and instead bang, she strikes him in the head."

Another reporter demanded, "How much did you win for the kid, Anthony?"

The attorney acknowledged the question with a nod, but continued on his track. "So when a complaint was filed against the woman for assault, the school fired this fine young man for what – for doing the right thing, for demanding justice – and then they went further, sending a letter to his school, telling them that he was fired for disobeying a direct order of the principal, and that he would not be invited back to teach."

There are murmurs of disgust among the reporters and on-lookers.

"I certainly showed them the error of their ways," said Bonifaccio, with just a touch of arrogance. "Not only did they pay – their insurance company did, of course – but they sent a letter to the young man's school, regaling him as a fine person who had done no wrong."

Several people on both sides of the crowd yelled out, "Right on!" "Go get 'em, Anthony!" They were two women, black, and suspiciously well-dressed, as though they might have been sent by the attorney's office.

"So how much, Anthony?" Butch asked again.

"Oh, please, it isn't about how much. But I will tell you that the entire amount was donated to the Roxbury Elementary Education Foundation."

"Even your fee?"

"My fee *and* my expenses."

"Mr. Bonifaccio," asked an out-of-town reporter, "does it disturb you when people say you're a racist for taking cases like this?"

Bonifaccio responded with what appeared to be cold fury, though those who knew him saw it for the performance it mostly was. "Me, a racist? My grandparents came to this country escaping Mussolini. They were called *wops*. Unable to speak English, only the lowest jobs were available to them. But they learned how to speak English. And they became American citizens. They worked hard. They taught me right. They never called themselves Italian-Americans. Yes, they were proud of their heritage, but they were more proud of being Americans."

He shifted to address another section of the gaggle. "This situation was never about skin color, at least not on the part of my client. Perhaps it was race that drove the school authorities to silence him, but race does not trump the truth. This was about right versus wrong. And this young man won a settlement based on what was – what is – right."

Chapter Eleven

Three hours later, Jeff Platen was, as usual, at his desk in the *Tribune* newsroom in New York, and not unusually, he was on the phone. On the other end of the call was his reporter, Zakim Nuran, on an Amtrak train on his way back from Boston to New York.

After reporting the essential details of the story to the editor, Zakim added, "I think you were right to send someone from New York to cover this, Jeff. There was certainly a lot of local energy in the air on this story. Not that it doesn't apply elsewhere, but you having me covering it is providing an appropriate distance for Allyson and her people."

"Good. I presume you checked the court filing?"

"Yes, as you suggested."

"It had everyone's names?"

"The grandmother's, Clarice Whyte, but not the grandson, as he is a minor."

"Good. If any of the local reporters choose to dig, they might find out who she is, but I don't know that they'll do that kind of digging."

"My guess, too, Jeff."

"How much was the settlement? It had to be registered

as it was a municipal payment, right."

"Yes, it was there. They got $10,000 for damages..."

"And?" the editor pressed.

"And $40,000 for punitive."

"Good for him. That lawyer really knew which two ribs to stick the knife between. A warning to anyone else kissing the wrong butt."

"Oh, there was also three grand in expenses, basically filing fees."

"Right. When will you have your piece to me, Zak?"

"Or where. I'm out of Providence. Maybe by Mystic, probably New London."

"Very clever."

"Should be to you in the next hour."

"Good. Stopping at the office?"

"That was my plan."

"Maybe get a beer."

"A better plan. See you around 4:30."

Chapter Twelve

Laurence Selden walked with Allyson Whyte on the National Seashore in Orleans on Cape Cod on an early fall afternoon. The weather was gorgeous. The Atlantic Ocean provided a delicious background sound, and the sea birds contributed their own shrill remarks.

"You're right, Allyson. The clam chowder at Land Ho! is the best I've ever had."

"It's long been a favorite of mine, Laurence. And whenever someone says they've had great clam chowder, I tell them they haven't had the best unless they've been there."

They walked without speaking for a few moments, making the transition back to work. Allyson said, "So you were telling me about your seminar before I arrived this morning, and what Charles Silberman had written."

"Yes," Laurence picked it up. "Silberman wrote a book called *Crisis in Black and White* which came out in 1964, even before the Civil Rights Act was passed. It is still amazingly prescient today. What I told the group this morning, and remember, these are all top thinkers about education with considerable classroom experience, but all now working outside of the system, is that Silberman made a critical distinction about the 20th century migration to the northern United States. The Europeans arrived with a different attitude towards assimilation because they knew they had to learn the language and the culture. But the blacks coming up from the south thought they were entitled in a way, because they spoke the language, though it was truly not the same as what we spoke here. And nor was their culture the same.

"Consider the conditions that the blacks had been living under in the south, and for two centuries. Their attitudes and expectations were far different from the immigrants from Europe. Particularly, their work ethic, as was their sense of personal responsibility."

Allyson took a deep breath and let it out through pursed lips. "That really does explain a lot, though it sounds, on the surface, as politically incorrect as one could imagine."

Laurence nodded. "That's one of the big problems with attempts at reform. We've seen it for the past 60 years in our cities where instead of going into the impoverished areas with a mandate to fix things, we have just put money in the hands of local leaders because we don't want to seem like we're telling the people what to do. Of course they don't know what to do with the money, and what to require of the people who receive it, so little has changed."

"From what I hear you saying," Allyson posited, "school bussing follows much the same road."

"That's right. Someone this morning brought up that point and said, frustration ringing in her voice, 'You can take the children out of the ghetto, but that doesn't take the ghetto out of the children.'"

"Oh my goodness."

"And of course, that's really the key to education... the early childhood. The environment and the parenting. By age three, a poor child will hear 30 million fewer words than a child brought up in a home of professionals."

"Can such ground be made up?"

"Sometimes, but imagine the stark change in circumstances that would be required."

"So what's to be done? Stop the poor and ignorant from having children. That's not going to happen."

"No, it's not. Nor can we take their children away from them, which means most of them remain in a cycle of poverty and ignorance, which also usually means violence."

They walked on in silence for a couple of minutes and then Allyson asked, "Surely there must be a solution?"

"Yes, of course. And instinctively, most teachers in the early grades know it and try to practice it. Which underscores how significant those first school years are – preschool, kindergarten, and first and second grades; ages three to six."

"This is where your concept of engagement comes in, Laurence?"

"Yes. The only people who can help these children get onto a track that shifts them out of the poverty cycle are the teachers who are able to make contact with them. With kindness, compassion, understanding, and most of all, instigating a sense of wonder. If they can ignite a child's curiosity, then they open up a channel that has thus far been closed or at least not used by them. And since it deals with the higher mind, it's significantly deeper than the survival-level connections that have been the child's life to date."

"Of course." Allyson was fascinated at the simplicity and critical value of what Laurence was explaining. She wondered aloud, "That's why we can recall the important teachers in our lives."

"Precisely." He said, pleased at how she made the connection. He added, "And not to sound too prosaic, but it is those teachers – in school and elsewhere, they can be a family member or a co-worker – they're the ones who touch our souls."

"And that doesn't happen nearly enough."

He stopped and looked at Allyson. "It only happens when the teacher knows how and chooses to reach in, and the child has an opening, one that he is not usually aware of."

"No wonder these early years are so vital. If you don't have a foundation, you have nothing on which to build the rest of your life."

"And if you don't know to build your own life, you look at people who have more than you with resentment, not incentive. De Toqueville wrote in *Democracy in America* almost 200 years ago, but this truth hasn't changed, that Americans have a tendency not to raise themselves up, but to pull their betters down."

They walked in silence again, Allyson taking in what Laurence had said. Then she said, "You talked this morning about there being another problem in teaching to the slowest students."

He nodded his head. "The lowest common denominator. This is another crippling approach done in the name of leveling the playing field. The problem is that when you are trying to teach healthy children – let's call them normal, and I only wish it were true – and you include the so-called special education children and the problem children in the same class, you are bound to fail the whole class. At the very least, you can't advance the normal children who are often bored out of their minds while the teacher works with the slower or disinclined children to bring them up to a higher level. Of course the special ed children will never have enough time and personal attention to" – he made quote marks in the air with his fingers – "catch up."

"When you speak of special ed, that category might include ESL?"

"I think of ESL differently but the issue is not dissimilar. The notion that children should learn a second language at the same time they are in regular studies is unreasonable, at best. They can't be expected to manage both at the same time. Children should first be taught English and then they can attend regular classes."

"And the problem children?"

"An unfortunate term, but when talking about schools running properly, those children are a problem. Those with mental health issues, or who are on drugs for hyperactivity, or those just angry, depressed, or violent...they are never going to do satisfactorily in this class because their problems aren't being dealt with."

"I read that American children are four times more likely to be on Ritalin or Adderall than European children."

"Yes, it's criminal. These children are almost always suffering from poor parenting – a lack of discipline and a lack of attention at home – or problems with siblings that the parents are unaware of or don't deal with them.

And very often it can be a matter of malnutrition."

Allyson shook her head. "And the schools are supposed to pick up the slack."

"Allyson, the primary purpose of schools is to prepare children to become healthy and productive members of society. They are the next generation to take full-fledged roles in society. Schools are where children need to learn about what it means to be adults."

"Then what is the role of their parents?"

"Aha, you've hit on one of the biggest obstacles in education. First, do you know what the root of the word education is?"

"I should, but I don't."

"That's all right. I don't think one in a hundred teachers in public school knows it. It's from the Latin word *educare* which means to lead from, as to lead from ignorance or lead from darkness. To lead from childhood to become a full-functioning member of the community."

"To lead from darkness. I like that. So what is the obstacle?"

"The parents. Not only do they not prepare the children for school – they don't read to them, even talk to them, teach them manners; they let the television babysit them – but they intervene in the schooling. They can interfere in their children's education in all sorts of ways. They do the children's homework for them, or don't help at all. They keep them up late. They don't encourage them to learn and to think for themselves.

"And there are those who go to the school and tax the teachers, frequently complaining about books their children are supposed to read. One group published their own version of *Huckleberry Finn* because Twain had used the word 'nigger' in it. And all too many parents object to what their children are taught in history. About what really happened. They prefer – and often demand – that a literal version of the Bible be taught instead."

"And some of the most dogmatic will get themselves on school boards where they wreak havoc."

"Yes. And one tragic result is that the teachers try to preempt the conflict with the parents by neutering their lessons. I've heard that some are not teaching their students about Martin Luther King, Jr., out of concern that it might generate complaints that will bring them up before the school administration."

Allyson shook her head. They had stopped walking. She said with a wry expression on her face, "You must be familiar with Twain's quote? 'In the first place, God made idiots. That was for practice. Then he made school boards.'"

Laurence laughed. "I'd forgotten that, but it is so true."

Allyson touched his shoulder. "I think I've taken too much of your time, Laurence, but it is so enriching."

"You are most gracious, Allyson, and you have not put me out a minute. However, I do have to head back, before the traffic gets impossible." They turned and started walking in the other direction. "But I think I would like to stop at the restaurant on the way back so I can bring home some more of that delicious clam chowder."

"Great minds... I was thinking the same thing."

Chapter Thirteen

Allyson walked through the newsroom and stopped at Drew's desk. With some effort he pulled his eyes away from his computer screen, saw who was there, and was immediately present with her.

"Hi," he said warmly.

"Hi, yourself," she responded with a chuckle. "I thought you'd like to know that New York has signed off on your Denver pieces."

"Fabulous."

"Jeff is having one of his fact-checkers go through them but he doesn't foresee any problems. He just wants to make sure that they are bulletproof."

Drew nodded his head sagely. "Good."

"You understand that there are some people who were already unhappy with your reporting, and the new pieces will have them really upset."

"Uh-huh."

"Virulently so."

"I guess."

"Don't guess, Drew. Good journalism produces enemies. You need to expect some pretty nasty comments, to you directly and on social media."

"Right."

"And if you receive any threats, or any communications that seem like threats, you need to bring them immediately to security. Let me know, but tell Oscar Satchell first. Even if you're not sure, they want to see everything that might be. Don't err on the side of maybe."

"Okay."

"Jeff has taken your email off the website, and he's alerted the other desks that there will likely be some fallout from the series."

Drew shook his head. "I didn't realize that people will find what we have to say so shocking. Or that they have a right to attack us for it. It's not like we're lying."

"They think you are. As we've seen over the last decade or so, especially since the Republicans welcomed the Tea Party people into their fold, facts and truth have fallen by the wayside. As has simple courtesy. Got it?"

"Yes, ma'am."

Allyson looked at him, not sure he fully realized his jeopardy, but at least she'd gotten his attention. "Okay, don't hesitate to call me if you have an issue. And if you sense any danger, call security if you're here, or 911."

"My god, you'd think we are starting a race war."

"Well maybe we are, but the sides are changing. So watch out. Your friends may not be as friendly as they were.

His demeanor changed. "You're making me nervous."

"Good, now you can get to work."

Chapter Fourteen

Clarice and Michael were sitting on a couch together in the den, having just watched the news coverage of the Bonifaccio news conference in front of the school. Clarice tapped the mute button and the sound of the news anchor went away.

"What did you think, grandma?"

She laughed. "Okay, I'll tell you first. I was glad you weren't there with him. I think it would have distracted from the message. He didn't seem too into himself; that was good. I also thought he handled the questions properly. What about you?"

"You were right that I shouldn't go. But maybe I could have stood in the back of the crowd and watched. No one would have known who I was."

"What do you think you missed just watching the news report?"

"Oh grandma, you know. They never cover the whole story. It's always he said-she said, like Mom says."

"Only this time the only 'she said' was the reporter saying the school district refused to comment. Smart of them, I have to think. They didn't really have a defense for what they did, and by remaining quiet —"

"They wouldn't let anyone identify them by their faces."

She smiled at her grandson. "You really are your parents' son, Michael. I think you have journalism in your blood."

Michael smiled back but with some sadness. "I wish Dad were home."

"You miss him a lot, I know. We all do."

He nodded. "Plus, I don't like him being in Afghanistan. No good is ever going to happen in that country. The Taliban, ISIS, the opium growers...they're all so primitive. No one is safe there, especially white people – Europeans and Americans."

"I know, Michael. It's a terrible place, but your father is careful. The western media people are fairly well protected."

"I know, Grandma, you told me that they have local reporters go out in the field while they prepare the coverage from inside the air base, but I still think it's too dangerous. Those people, they play by different rules."

Clarice sat quietly, gently rubbing Michael's neck. After a while she asked him, "Do you think you would want to go to a war zone if you become a reporter?"

He winced and then chuckled. "You mean like Roxbury?"

Laughing, "Oh, Michael, you're so bad."

He sighed. "You know, Grandma, it's not about where it's safe. I would want to be where I could make a difference. I don't think Afghanistan or Somalia or Haiti or places like that will maybe ever become peaceful. Their cultures are too polarized or corrupt. I'd rather be in places where change is possible."

Clarice looked at her grandson with quiet pride. "There's a lot to be done here in our country, isn't there?"

"Yes, and here more than most places, change is possible. The big thing is getting people to understand what the challenges are, and how when we think and work together, we can fix what's broken."

Chapter Fifteen

Allyson was standing in a one-room schoolhouse with Mary Ellen Slayburns, the great-granddaughter of a woman who taught in that room.

Angela said, "It's hard to conceive of what school was like in those days, the early years of the 20th century."

"Indeed," responded Mary Ellen. "I went through my grandmother's attic where she had kept all of the textbooks she used, the tests that she gave, report cards, and some of the newspapers of that time with the major headlines."

"Also her diary, you told me."

"Yes, she was a dedicated diarist. For the 34 years that she was a teacher. She started in the last year of the presidency of Theodore Roosevelt, the fall of 1908, and retired at 54 – she was suffering from rheumatism – just after the war in the Pacific was turning. In her diary she noted that the graduation that year occurred a month after the battle of Midway which was in June of 1942."

"So she must have seen significant changes in schools over those more than three decades."

"In the schools, and in the country. Those years were, as she saw it, the birth of the United States as an international leader. She was very proud then, though as she told my mother in her later years, she was not happy with the direction the country was taking. She lived to be 92, so she was witness to the Cold War and Vietnam."

"But she also lived through the civil rights era, and the beginning of the women's liberation movement."

Mary Ellen smiled. "Yes, she did. I was born in 1960, and I can remember her talking about the good changes. She said she hoped we would be able to keep up with the changes, and not lose our human values."

"The photographs you have from that era tell a lot, don't they?"

Mary Ellen, "Yes they do. The children were far better behaved. Not because my great-grandmom would rap their knuckles with a ruler, something that happened very infrequently, but because they knew that they would get worse from their parents. Remember, their families were giving up a primary source of day labor on their farms or in their stores. It was a big sacrifice, the purpose of which was to give their children a better life – the skills to move the family business forward, or to go out on their own and find success."

"When did things begin to change?"

"Nana said it was after the war ended. There was a great sense of victory, of the United States being the world savior, that the war wasn't fought on our soil, for the most part. She said when the soldiers came home, they got jobs and started families, and they were all about giving their children growing up what was beyond their parents means." The sunny disposition on Mary Ellen's face clouded over.

"But that seemed to mean caring too much for their

children. Or maybe that's not the right way to say it. They maybe protected them too much."

"The precursor to the helicopter parents?" Allyson asked.

Mary Ellen nodded. "Something like that. They demanded less of their children, I think was what it was. They did more for them. Their children didn't have to work as hard. Going to school became what you did rather than seeing it as the opportunity – of a lifetime – to grow yourself." She peered at Allyson. "Does that make sense, because I'm interpreting what I heard from my great-grandmother and my mother." She demurred, "I didn't really know my grandmother. She had a falling out with the family and moved to a commune in Oregon years ago."

"I think it is, sadly. I don't think your great-grandmother would have enjoyed being a teacher in the Sixties. Or no, she might have found the Sixties exciting, but later it would have been a different kind of challenge, to keep the children's attention."

There was a long silence as Allyson walked slowly about the room, looking at the historic photographs on the wall and feeling the ghosts of a century ago. She turned back to the other woman.

"Why do you suppose we let go the value of an education? Why we stopped seeing how important it was to be bright? Why we scorned the 'eggheads'?" She heard the anger and despair in her voice, but her face made it clear that the focus was on those who didn't treasure what had happened in that schoolroom.

Mary Ellen shared the distress, a fourth generation observing the deterioration. "Great-grandmom thought it might have been laziness. I don't know. My mother spent many hours with me making sure that I not only did my homework, and did it well, but that I understood what I was being taught, both the facts but especially the context. Why what I was studying was important, or it should be. There wasn't much of that in my school. We just digested what was in the textbooks without fitting the ideas into our own lives." She stopped and drew a breath. "That's why I've home-schooled our two children."

"How is that for you, if I might ask?"

The smile returned. "Oh I love it. The children are sponges, soaking up all that I put in front of them. And they never run out of questions to ask me about what they're studying. Especially about history, they keep asking why we did things the way we did, or how it would have been better another way. They love history. It's like a mystery or a drama for them."

"What about other subjects? Like arithmetic, which so many children seem to struggle with?" And she asked, "How old are your children?"

"I have two boys," she said proudly, "ten and twelve. And they both have done so well with arithmetic that we have moved into higher level math. They really got into it because I made it about life. You know, with opening a savings account, telling them about budgets and credit cards. They saw how important it would be in their lives to know how these things worked."

"Were there any subjects they didn't like?"

Mary Ellen's smile broadened. "Foreign languages. No, they liked them. Brad wanted to learn French because so many people in the northeast have French ancestry, but

Todd preferred Spanish since there were so many immigrants from south of the border, and he was planning to move to California."

"Very smart."

"Todd is a tech genius. I told him he was more likely to be using Chinese in his field. And he agreed. So the boys study their own language, and they're learning to talk to each other, Brad in French and Todd in Mandarin."

"That must make it interesting for the home-schooling mom," Allyson said with admiration.

"Oh, it's a blast. I'm learning a little of both languages. Not enough so that it's useful, at least not yet, but it feels good to be able to say a few things the way people in other societies express themselves. And I know our family will want to travel together to France and China. And who knows where else?"

Chapter Sixteen

Michael and Fiona were sitting behind a counter on stools inside a booth they had set up on the main street in the town of Exeter, New Hampshire. A banner at the top of the booth read "Making School Better." People were coming up to the booth, first to ask questions, and then to give answers.

A pretty, red-haired prep school senior with glasses, Fiona wore a white shirt under a maroon school blazer and a conservative grey plaid skirt. Michael was wearing a similar blazer, white shirt, and navy tie.

Fiona was explaining to an older couple the purpose of the booth. "We are collecting ideas from people about how to make schools better."

The man smiled, and pointing upward said, "To wit, your banner."

"Exactly."

"What are you going to do with the ideas you get?"

"We're going to write them up in a report for our current events class."

The man nodded. "Okay, here's something for you. I think that starting in grammar school, students should be taught about life. How it works. What it means to be a good citizen. How important it is to be smart and to not waste their precious time learning."

Michael was recording the man's comments. He turned to the woman. "Have you any ideas about how to make schools better?"

"I certainly do. I think boys should have to take home ec, home economics. They should learn about living on a budget, shopping, keeping a home, the basics of cooking."

The man nodded his agreement. "And knowing the difference between renting and buying, understanding hidden costs and what you can really afford instead of going into debt."

The woman added, "And the importance of being thrifty, and saving for a rainy day."

"Wow," said Fiona. "That's great!"

"Why thank you, young lady," the woman said, and then to the man, "Come along, dear. Let's not take up all of their time." They nodded to the students and walked off.

A woman in a business suit stopped in front of the booth. "I'll tell you how to make schools better. Have more discipline. The students today are out of control. They don't pay attention to the classes; they don't obey their teachers. It's hard enough to teach, but when the children misbehave, it's chaos. You can't learn in such an environment. It's the parents' fault. They should be fined for raising children who are disruptive in the classroom." With that she walked off.

Michael and Fiona looked at each other with raised eyebrows. Fiona opened her notebook wrote about what the woman had said. When she looked up, she saw three teenage boys looking over at the booth from across the street. Their hair slicked down, they were wearing tee shirts with a pack of cigarettes in the turned-up sleeves. "Townies," she said to Michael under her breath.

They watched as the boys sauntered across the street toward the booth, making the traffic stop for them. There was a haughty, challenging style to their walk and expressions. When they got to the booth, the boy in the middle of the three, sneering at Fiona, asked, "So what's all this about?"

"We're asking people what would make schools work better, especially for students?" she replied evenly.

"How 'bout closing 'em?" the boy said, scoffing, his friends joining in the laughter.

She waited until they quieted down and then answered. "The problem is that people who don't make it through high school lose out. They have trouble getting even poor jobs. Many of them wind up on drugs or become alcoholics. Their relationships fail. They often land in jail."

"Whereas people who take school seriously," Michael put in, "find good jobs and live better, healthier lives in good relationships. They get to call their own shots."

Seeing annoyance on the brow of the middle boy, Fiona said to him, "What could have been done to make school more valuable to you? Was it boring? Was what they were teaching not important to you?"

"Yeah," said one of the other boys. "It didn't mean anything, you know? It was like all about what happened hundreds of years ago. So what?"

Michael showed him interest, "And they never told you why that mattered? How the people back then made decisions and wrote laws that are affecting us today?"

The boy looked surprised. He shook his head.

Fiona turned to the third boy. "What about you? What would have made a difference to you in school?"

The middle boy butted in. "More recess." He laughed, but the other boys were less interested in his joke.

The third boy said, "I would have liked more time in shop, and working with my hands. I always wanted to work on cars. I didn't care about all that other stuff ...English and stuff."

The first boy nodded his head, "No kidding. They should teach us what we need to know, about what we want to do."

Fiona looked the middle boy in the eyes. "What do you want to do? What do you want to be doing in ten years?"

He appeared offended at having been asked a question to which he didn't have an answer. It was obvious that he hadn't thought about it. "I don't know," he snarled but weakly. "Get a job, I guess."

Fiona asked gently, "What if you could choose any job? What would it be? And what would you need to know to do that job well?" She paused. "That's why we're asking these questions so that people will learn what they need to, so they can have the lives they want to live."

The boy was overwhelmed. "Aw. Come on," he said to his friends. "I don't have time for this." They were slow to follow him away. The last boy looked back over his shoulder, his expression suggesting that he'd heard something important.

Michael and Fiona watched them walk away. "That was interesting," he observed. She agreed.

A policeman came ambling down the sidewalk, looking in store windows, keeping the peace. He came to a stop in front of the booth. "So what is this all about?" he asked the two of them pleasantly.

"We're asking people what might be done for schools to do a better job of giving people a good education," Fiona explained.

Michael told him, "There are plenty of experts who have ideas, about what works and what doesn't, but we want to hear from people who aren't experts. People the decision-makers don't usually ask."

"That makes sense," the policeman said, interested.

"What about you?" Fiona asked. "What do you think schools might do differently?"

The policeman tilted his head back in thought, and then through a narrowed gaze answered them. "You know what I think schools could do better at? They could teach children more about other children, about how different people are. And, you know, not that people are bad or good, but they come from different places and they know different things." He paused for a moment and then finished his thought. "They should teach that you do a lot better in life if you listen a little more, and judge a little less. You can meet some very interesting people that way. You can learn a lot."

Fiona and Michael looked intently at the policemen. Finally Fiona asked, curious, "How did you figure that out?"

The Bright Wise Solution

The policeman chuckled. "I guess it was pretty much on-the-job training. When I joined the force 15 years ago, with an associate's degree, I was pretty sure I knew everything. And pretty quick there, I found out I didn't know anything. I was always being surprised by people, for worse and better. So I listened more. I asked more questions. I saw that when I thought I knew people by how they looked, and even how they acted, there was always something I didn't know about them that was important to whatever was going on. The situation wasn't so cut-'n-dry."

"Excuse me for saying, sir," Michael said, "but it sounds like you should be training the new policemen."

The man chuckled again. "Yeah, funny you should say that. The chief wants the new guys to learn by the rule book and policy manual, but he winds up sending them out with me for the first six months." He nodded at the two students. "This is good what you're asking. I hope you can do something with it." With a half-salute to them, he continued his rounds.

"This is really great, Michael," Fiona said, excitement in her voice.

Michael nodded. "I never thought that people would speak so openly about this."

"Maybe because everyone went to school."

"And they didn't have such a great experience."

"Hello, Fiona...Michael."

The two turned to see a well-appointed gentleman in his mid-fifties who had come from the other direction that they had been facing.

Surprised, they managed to say together, "Hello, Head-

The Bright Wise Solution

master."

"I thought I should stop by and see how two of my favorite seniors are doing on their fall project."

They two looked at each other, Michael giving an almost imperceptible nod to Fiona.

"Sir, this has been fantastic," she said. "Everyone who has stopped here has had something important to say."

"Even three town – I mean, local boys," Michel put in. "They told us a lot of what they were taught didn't mean anything to them."

"History," Fiona inserted.

"It wasn't made relevant to them," Michael finished.

"They also gave us the impression that they would have done well in a vocational training program."

The headmaster nodded his head. "No doubt many students would echo both those observations, especially those who didn't have a more cultivated hunger to learn more."

The two students nodded their heads enthusiastically.

"Please let me see your reports when they are done. I think all schools will have something to gain from what you are learning."

Chapter Seventeen

The next morning, though there was no connection to what happened in nearby Exeter, Anthony Bonifaccio drove up to Hanover, New Hampshire. For two reasons. One was because he was on the board of the Dartmouth Fraternity Society that was having their annual meeting, and the other was to have lunch with Clarice Whyte at the Pine, an upscale restaurant whose prices attracted more alums than students. The two had no agenda. It was merely that they had found each other to be something of odd kindred spirits who shared a strong interest in helping right to prevail.

"I think we're in trouble, Clarice. There aren't nearly enough people in the pipeline like your grandson."

"That's kind of you to say, Anthony. I wish I could disagree with you. I think his grandparents had a significant role in making him the young man he is, the man he is going to be, but his parents really deserve most of the credit. I think it's always about the parenting. And probably from before conception. Who these people are, why they want to bring a child into this world, into their lives, and what they are going to contribute to his growth."

"And how many people do you think ask themselves these questions, talk with the other person to get answers...and the right answers? I read that 50% of the births in this country are unwanted or unplanned. That's hardly a good first step. I've also read that the fetus knows if it isn't wanted. That's one of the reasons that adopted children often don't do very well."

The waiter arrived at the table and handed them menus. "May I offer you something to drink, Mr. Bonifaccio? Ma'am?"

"Hah," said Clarice with a laugh. "I work in this town, Anthony, and you are more familiar here than I am."

He laughed.

"And yes, I think a preprandial libation might be just the thing, considering the tenor of our conversation even before we've ordered." She looked at the waiter. "A Bloody Mary, please, and moderately spicy."

"The same for me, Ivan, please, but save the vegetables. More room for the drink."

Ivan nodded to them and left the table.

"Okay, Anthony, we surely won't be able to limit births to bright, conscious people who have the resources to pour into child-rearing, which means we have to make up for the parents in school."

"Clarice, do you know Susan Jacoby's work?"

"I saw her piece called *Stop Apologizing for Being Elite* in the paper the other day. Very powerful. And timely. It tied in very well with the conversation Michael and I had with the Boston police lieutenant that I told you about."

"I remember you telling me about her. Very impressive." He shook his head. "We are drowning in a victimhood culture. We're all about rights and virtually unaware that we also have responsibilities."

"Can that be reversed through education?"

"Through education, yes. Some people. Though by the time children get to school, for many of them it's a real challenge to turn them around from what was instilled in them in their early childhood."

Ivan appeared and put the drinks down before them. "Have you decided what you would like for lunch?"

"Give us some more time, would you, Ivan? I'll wave you down when we've looked at the menu."

"Very good, Mr. Bonifaccio."

"I'm sorry, Clarice, I should have asked you first if you are starving."

"No, Anthony, I'm fine. Thank you." She cocked her head, "I just remembered Twain's comment about not letting school get in the way of education."

"Even then it was obvious. Yes, Jacoby wrote a book *The Age of American Unreason* in 2008 which explains why we are so off track with our schooling. It's been a struggle for two hundred years between the intellectuals and the religionists, particularly the evangelicals and fundamentalists. Those who would prefer that the only book in school is the Bible. They fight tooth and nail to keep any and all discussion of evolution out of the classroom, and relent only when they can insist on having creationism taught at the same time.

"Jacoby noted that there's been a dangerous rise in anti-intellectualism over the last forty-five years or so, and it has dumbed down our country so that not only does a third of the population believe in the literal interpretation of the Bible, but they put religion above civil rights, and even above the Constitution. And this narrow thinking has discouraged free thinking and informed discussion of climate change, health care, the economy, education, and good government. Ironically, it has compromised our basic human values of honesty and compassion.

"By the way, she has just published another book called *The Age of American Unreason in a Culture of Lies*. I presume it updates the downward spiral over the past decade, but I haven't read it yet."

Clarice had no immediate response, but Anthony knew he'd said enough.

"Have I taken away your appetite, Clarice?" he asked her, only half-joking.

With her elbows on the table in front of her, she had steepled her fingertips in front of her mouth. "No, Anthony. Quite the contrary. I'm riled. If there is one force I will not be cowed by, it is the closed minds that want to spread ignorance and fear. I don't know what is to be done, but I know I can think better with some food in my stomach." With that she picked up the menu.

Anthony peered at her from across the table, not replying, nor did he reach for his menu.

"Not hungry, Anthony?" she asked him.

He shook his head thoughtfully. "I mean, yes, I'm hungry, but I already know what I want to eat." He raised his hand slightly and soon Ivan was at the table taking their order.

"Clarice, you sound so strong, considering what I just said. More than strong. You're ready to man the barricades."

"Not man the barricades, Anthony. That's a defensive posture. I want to attack. I want to bring the leaders of this nonsense down in a way that their flocks bleat and bah their way to sanity. I will not be a party to the collapse of our magnificent country. I will not be silent. America is a synthesis of the East and West. We were founded, not just to be a country, but as a symbol of what man is capable of, and when I go, I want to know that we're on the path to see our destiny realized."

It was Anthony's turn for silence, but it wasn't long before he broke out of it. "Sure you don't want a martini or something?"

She smiled at her friend. "Anthony, I remember hearing about Abraham Maslow talking to high school age students and asking them, 'Who among you is going to be great?' Of course, none of them raised their hands. And he said, 'Who else then?'"

"Yes, I had forgotten that. That's huge."

"Well there's another piece that goes with that. A prequel, if you will, and that is you stand before a large group of young, new parents, and you ask them, 'Who among your children is going to be great?' And you've got to think that every hand in the room will shoot up. That tells you something. It tells you there's room to intervene. There's a way to reach these kids who are our next generation of leaders, and dammit, that's what we're going to do."

Anthony cocked his head. "This might be relevant to what you're saying, Clarice. One of my Dartmouth alum friends said something about a group of professors from around the country working on a new educational project. It has to do with developing a national curriculum. It's a project funded by some uber wealthy individuals who have remained mostly behind the scenes because they don't want critics to use them as targets to divert attention from what's being produced. As so often happens. Kill the messenger. I'll find out more about it."

Chapter Eighteen

As was her practice every quarter, Allyson Whyte trained down to New York to get face time – she thoroughly disliked the term – with Jeff Platen and to confirm expenses and budgets for the New England bureau with the *Tribune* financial overseers. As she walked out of her last meeting at which her numbers had correlated with their projections, she was looking forward to her time with the domestic editor. They not only had a good working relationship based on performance and trust, but as something of a mentor to her, he in fact, if not deliberately, kept her edge sharpened.

But now as he looked up at her from his desk as he was on the phone, his expression was serious. She knew that look; she'd seen it all too many times before. He was getting bad news. Immediately she felt the icy grasp of fear and pulled out her phone. She hadn't turned it off, but what if there had been a call from Michael? She checked and saw there were no calls that would have needed her attention.

Her eyes went back to the editor. He had seen her response to him and realized it had frightened her. He held up a palm toward her and shook his head. She nodded and slowed her pace toward him so that he might finish his call before she reached his desk. It didn't take long.

Jeff stood up behind his desk. He was shaking his head. Allyson looked at him. She didn't have to ask him to tell her what happened.

"Your friend, Selden..."

"Yes, he's in town. Working with a school in the Bronx. He's really turned it around." But she knew that didn't fit what he had to tell. She winced.

"Allyson, he's been hurt. Someone who'd been fired showed up at a meeting with a gun."

"Oh god no. Tell me he's all right. Please."

"I don't know how all right he is. He's alive. He has been taken to Columbia Presbyterian. They're very good."

"Oh my god," she said plaintively, and then anger flooded her heart. "There is no god! That's why they only shoot the good ones."

He pulled her to him and she yielded easily. He patted her on the back. "Don't get too upset until we find out it's appropriate. I was told it was a small caliber pistol, fired by a woman, so I think we might hold our worry until we learn more."

Allyson pushed back gently against his grasp and he let her go. She took a step back, and suddenly the reporter, she looked at him with curiosity. "What does it mean that it was fired by a woman?"

"Ah," said Jeff, chuckling. "Sit," he commanded, gently but firmly as he gestured to the chair in front of his desk and took his own seat. She acceded.

"First of all, let us be glad that it was a small caliber - pistol."

She didn't say anything. He looked at her in a way that demanded a response. She nodded her head slowly.

"Second, the stats are overwhelming that women who are firing a gun from an emotional state, as this woman obviously was, are struggling with their feelings and are far less likely to aim right. They aren't sure that they want to actually shoot someone, and their coordination is shaky, literally."

Allyson looked at him skeptically. "Is that true? I mean about the statistics."

Jeff, eyebrows raised, replied, "Yeah. And in this case, thank goodness."

"How do you know what happened? About the shooting, I mean."

"The city desk got the call from the responding precinct. They'd seen one of your pieces, or Drew's, that mentioned Selden, and they called me."

"What else do we know?"

"At the moment, just that someone –" he smiled – "a woman, who had been given her notice, went into a conference room and fired a shot. I don't know if she was aiming at Selden, or if she thought he was responsible, but he was shot. I don't know where he was struck."

"What happened to the woman?"

"Someone grabbed her and held her for the police."

Allyson sat looking at nothing in front of her, nodding her head slowly. When she stopped and looked up at her editor she said, "I hope he's all right, Jeff. He's really a very fine man. So bright. Doing so much to change our failing education system."

The Bright Wise Solution

Jeff nodded, then he shrugged. "Well, we have every reason to be optimistic. I think." And he shrugged again.

"Can you call the hospital?"

"Yeah," he said. He reached over, picked up the phone, and pressed a button. After a moment he said, "Rachel, would you please find me someone at Columbia Presbyterian who can tell me the condition of the man they brought in with the gunshot in the South Bronx?"

He listened. "I know. He was a consultant and he was at the school where they got their scores turned around." He listened. "Yes, that's the one. Thanks. When you have someone, put him through to me."

He hung up the phone. "It won't be a minute," he assured Allyson, and it was less than that. The intercom line buzzed, he picked it up, listened and said, "Good. Thank you, Rachel." And after a moment, "Dr. Goodlight, Jeff Platen. What can you tell me, please, about Laurence Selden? I'm not looking for a news story. We have reported on his work in the past, and our New England bureau chief is with me. She knows him and has written about him." He listened and very quickly relief wrote itself on his face. "That's very good news, Doctor, thank you. When will he – ." He stopped and soon spoke again. "Great. Okay. If you might let him know that Allyson Whyte called about him...That's right. She'll call him directly. She has his cell number." He didn't need to confirm that with Allyson – he knew she would – but she nodded anyway. "Thanks again. You folks do such great work up there." He nodded and then hung up.

"Phew," he said to Allyson. "A very minor flesh wound. The bullet went between his left arm and chest, cutting both but only slightly. He's been patched up, given some painkillers, and in an hour or so will be sent home. Or back to his hotel. The doctor said he couldn't tell me which hotel, but I'm sure you can find out."

A smile of gratitude rose slowly on Allyson's face. She looked at Jeff for a long moment without saying anything. Then she said, "Thank goodness it was a woman."

Chapter Nineteen

"I'd give you a hug, Laurence," Allyson said as she closed in on him in the lobby of the Carlyle Hotel, "But I might cause you pain."

Laurence held out his right hand toward Allyson and she took gentle hold of it. "I'm really all right. More than scratched, but not quite wounded. And they gave me a large supply of pain pills."

"I'm so sorry, my friend, and glad that I could see you with my own eyes to know that you will be around for a while."

"At least for the dinner you promised me."

"Perfect," she said, and they walked together to The Carlyle Restaurant.

"This is on your expense account, I trust," he said as they were presented the menus.

"Yes, I got it approved when they knew you were on drugs that would prevent you from drinking wine."

Laurence chuckled and it caused him to grimace.

"Oh, Laurence, how thoughtless of me to make you laugh. It causes you pain."

"My dear, I may briefly abstain from the fruit of the vine

but never from humor. Please."

"Very good choice."

"Are you up to telling me what got you into this situation that you would have to choose?"

He sighed. "Yes, but let's decide on our food first. I have to find something I can manage with just a fork."

"Of course, though I know they would be glad to cut whatever you really want into bite-size pieces. It's hard to find an establishment anywhere in this city that makes a more serious effort to take care of their guests' needs."

"That's right, of course. And why I stay here every time I'm in The City. Plus it's not ten minutes from The Met. I can always get my fine art fix."

"It is magnificent. I wonder...well, we can talk about that later. First we order, then you tell me what happened to you, and then art."

They perused the menu and when Allyson saw that Laurence had made his selections, she raised her eyes to the waiter who had been watching them and he came to their table. He took their order and left.

Laurence smiled at Allyson. "I like some of this new world." He saw the question in her face. "Where the woman can take charge at dinner. The way you subtly brought the waiter to take our order. I always took care of it, and tonight I didn't have to. Thank you."

"You are a special man, Laurence. Not feeling you're being eclipsed. I intervened, so to say, so that you wouldn't have to raise your arm."

He chuckled lightly but with no indication of pain. In answer to her obvious interest he said, "I think the meds are kicking in."

She nodded.

He took a deep breath, testing his rib cage, and let it out. "Yes, much better. So now it's time to sing for my supper."

"Only if it won't be a strain, emotionally or physically."

"Of course not. I don't think you know that I was in the military."

"I didn't but I did notice your bearing."

"I was in the Marines, saw action in Vietnam in 1967 and '68."

Allyson frowned. Without knowing where the question came from she asked, "Is that what saved you today?"

He looked at her with surprise. "How strange. I hadn't thought about that, but yes, it probably did." He took another deep breath and let it out quietly through pursed lips. "Amazing that you should ask, and I shouldn't have thought about it." He shook his head. "But enough of what we don't know, I will tell you what happened.

"I was at the Grand Concourse High School. I think you know that it is a turn-around story from low academic scores and serious behavior problems to one of the safest high schools in the Bronx and with grades climbing every year for the past four years."

"I did read about it. Much of it attributable to the program you persuaded the school administration to implement."

"Yes, it did work well. In part because the city had given up on it, and allowed it to charter, and also because I had five key administrators who knew how to manage the teachers, the students, and especially the parents. They were able to get people to give us a shot – oh, wrong word – the opportunity to prove that we could engage the students. We asked for two years, but we were so successful in just the first six months – the difference was obvious and positive – that we were able to implement the rest of our plans sooner than we had expected."

"And from what I read, you were not only successful, but it was by following the format and schedule that you had first laid out to all of the participants. Transparency."

Laurence nodded. "That was a big piece of it, yes." He paused as the waiter came with a garden salad for Allyson and a butternut squash bisque for him. He tasted the soup and enjoyed it. "Another good reason for coming to New York."

"Please go ahead and eat, Laurence. Your story can wait."

"Thank you. I'll do both." And after another two spoonfuls, he put the spoon down and continued with his story.

"I was down here today to talk with the department heads about some tweaking of the curriculum for the spring semester. I could have done it by email, but I find it's more effective to speak directly with these people. It is then that I can pick up any issues that aren't verbalized."

"Of course."

"And there is that incredible *Streams and Mountains China* exhibit at the Met that I can't seem to get enough of. Anyway, we had just finished our session this afternoon

The Bright Wise Solution

and I was talking to the head of counseling. He's a man I've known for probably twenty years. Bright, talented guy, we have worked together at four different schools. He was explaining to me why he had to let go his assistant, a woman who had not worked out for a variety of reasons and was given her notice a few weeks before her probationary period was up. But she was being paid through the rest of the term, and he'd given her a positive exit letter.

"But suddenly I saw him looking past me and there was fear in his eyes. I had a sense that it was this woman behind me, and I turned around slowly and deliberately. And there she was, a young Asian woman, looking sort of disheveled, and holding a small revolver in both hands, pointing it at my colleague. Thinking she wouldn't fire if I was in the way, I moved over in front of him. But she let out a howl that I can only describe as that of a wounded animal, and then she fired. The bullet caught me between my left bicep and my fourth rib."

"Oh my goodness, Laurence. You were lucky."

"Uh, yes, I suppose so." He smiled. "Yes, of course. And also that there was no one behind me. The bullet went into the wall."

"And?"

"Her arm with the gun fell down at her side and her other hand she clapped over her mouth. One of the faculty members grabbed her arm with the gun and pulled the revolver from her hand. Another fellow pulled her arms behind her and forced her to the floor. Someone called the police, and the school nurse was summoned. She cut off my coat and shirt and applied bandages to my two wounds to stop the bleeding. An ambulance arrived not ten minutes later, and they took me across the river to the Columbia Presbyterian ER, where they cleaned up everything, and x-rayed me to confirm there was no bone damage or bullet fragments. Shot me full of pain killer – it did hurt – and then kept watch on me for a couple of hours to make sure I wouldn't suffer some sort of aftereffect. I didn't. The police questioned me. I told them what I knew; you called around that time. And then I was released to go back to my hotel. One of the hospital executives sent me back here in his car."

"Finish your bisque, Laurence, and then I have some questions."

He did and she did, one of which was how he now saw his Marine experience in what happened.

Laurence took a deep breath and let it out slowly. "I was a captain in my last year in Vietnam. I saw the absolute worst of human behavior, on both sides. My unit was one of the first to go into My Lai and see the carnage done by our troops."

"Oh my god. I don't know how anyone could have gotten over that. And I just saw some of the Haberle photographs."

Laurence nodded.

"We were in a bar in Da Nang not long after. One of my men – a kid, maybe 18, but you became a man quickly in Vietnam – got drunk. He confronted one of the non-coms who was in Calley's unit. The kid was crying – bawling – and suddenly he had his .45 out, hammer back, and pointed at the man. I walked slowly in front of him, maybe two feet from the muzzle of his gun." Laurence paused, choked though not visibly, by the memories of that moment.

Allyson waited, saying nothing, keeping her face blank.

Laurence finished the story. "And then the kid stopped bawling. He sniffed once. Then put the muzzle of his gun against his temple and pulled the trigger."

"Oh dear god, no," Allyson said, and tears poured down her cheeks.

Chapter Twenty

Allyson called Laurence the next morning just before she left for the train station to return to Boston. She always traveled by train to New York if there wasn't some urgency for her arrival. It was a far calmer trip on the ground, more comfortable, easier to work, and she had already done enough flying in her career.

"How are you feeling this morning?"

"Worse, of course, but it was to be expected. The body has entered its full-on healing effort, or so the doctor explained it."

"Not to return to that difficult subject, but were you ever wounded when you were a Marine? Physically?" she added.

"I'm sorry I told you that story, Allyson. I can't remember telling anyone else since I got back." He paused and said, "It's a reflection of how much I value our relationship."

Allyson sniffed involuntarily. "Me, too, Laurence."

"As regards your question," he said, to move the conversation past the rough patch, "Ironically in the 18 months I was in that god-forsaken war, I was never wounded. I was bumped trying to stop a runaway jeep, but all I got was a bruise on my hip."

Allyson laughed. "A story for another time."

"Yes. So have yourself a nice ride up to Boston."

"Feel better, my dear friend."

There was a long pause on the other end of the line. "Your audience, and friendship, has encouraged me, Allyson, to move my work along with more vigor. We have work to do. We will move the ball forward, as they say."

Chapter Twenty-One

Drew and Allyson met in the lobby of their office building, as she was coming from South Station, and he from Logan airport having just flown in on an early flight from Denver. Each had a travel bag over their shoulder.

"I heard about Laurence. He's going to be all right?" he asked, obvious concern on his face.

"Yes, thank goodness. The bullet had eyes and just tore some skin," she replied. "How was Aurora?"

"It turned out to be an even more valuable trip than I expected. I got a lot more information that is going to add a significant new dimension to our story."

"Good. When can you write me up a precis of what you got?"

"Let me get settled and grab a sandwich. Maybe half an hour?"

Allyson laughed. "Please have yourself a decent lunch, Drew. This afternoon will be fine."

"You got it."

And she did, less than an hour later. Allyson read the precis, and had anyone been watching her, they would have seen her raising her eyebrows and shaking her head any number of times as she read through the one-pager, underlining in several places. Then she got up and walked over to Drew's desk.

"You're right. You've got a lot. It's awful, and from what you seem to have found online, Aurora is hardly unique."

"The private schools and Catholic schools do considerably better," Drew said, "at least in terms of national testing scores and behavior. Far fewer arrests, of course, because they can be selective about who they let in, and they are quicker to toss someone who doesn't fit in, though there's not a lot of that.

"And the public schools, instead of sending home students suspended for misbehaving, they will keep them at the school, in a separate room, because the state pays them on the basis of the number of seats they fill on a daily basis."

Allyson looked grim. "And that also skews the stats on attendance and behavioral problems. So the school district looks like they're doing a better job than they're really doing, and the schools look safer than they really are?"

Drew shrugged. "They're running the public schools like a business. Not that the private schools aren't, but at least those parents have a pretty good idea what's going on. And for the Catholic schools, the parents are generally responsible for the compliance of their children."

Allyson looked back at the one-pager. "You don't talk about charter schools."

"It's hard to find good statistics, in test scores or behavior. They're mostly new though spreading, but there hasn't been enough time to weigh them clearly, especially compared to public schools."

"And a big issue," Allyson put in, "is that they don't accept everyone who comes to the door."

"A very big issue. Some of them get criticized for not taking autistic children or those with other learning disabilities."

"What do you think about that, Drew?"

"Mmm. At the risk of sounding elitist, the wrong kind of elitist, I think that not everyone should go to the same schools. That trying to raise every child tends to lower the bar, and the best and the brightest, and most of those in the middle, tend not to get the education they seek.

"I remember reading a story in the *Chronicle* a while back how they took a dozen high school juniors who should have been doing better than they were in school, over the summer they put them in jobs in different San Francisco businesses, and they all thrived. All of them. They were engaged in the real world and they'd had enough of classes that they found boring or irrelevant."

"That says a lot, doesn't it?"

"It does. As far as the children who aren't up to the task, yes, they should be looked after, but not everyone is going to do well in the same type of school. Some people just need a little more help; maybe their grammar school – or their parenting – wasn't up to snuff. In my junior high school, seventh through ninth grade, they broke us down into the top students, the middle, and those who needed extra help. I thought that made a lot of sense."

"And what about those who needed more than extra help?"

Drew shrugged again, not without empathy. "I don't

know if there is a fix for the children with mental disabilities. There was a situation in Ohio a few years back where the parents sued the school district or the state to educate their mentally disabled child at a cost of over $50,000 a year when the average per student expenditure was like $11,000. I'm sorry for the parents, and the kid, for that matter, but that kid never had a future. The thing is that not everyone gets to do everything, especially when it will cost other children – those who actually do have a future – for whom the education means something."

"I certainly can't argue with that. The money's not there, and even if it were, how would we set limits? And what do the parents do? I don't know. It's the fear of every parent that their child will be special but in a very real and sad way."

"That's one of the reasons why a number of my male – obviously – friends have gotten vasectomies."

"Really?" Allyson was surprised.

"They don't want any children. Beyond the risk that there might be something wrong with them. They're not interested in being fathers, at least not now."

"Would they think of getting them reversed, if you don't mind my asking?"

"They – we, actually; a lot of us – know that we don't want to have children, period. I know it's possible in most cases to reverse a vasectomy, but of the men I've talked to, and some women, too, there is little interest in adopting. The numbers aren't very good on that score for having a normal, healthy child."

Allyson nodded. "So I understand. It underscores that

tragedy of unwanted children, caused in part by religious opprobrium but also so many people just take chances."

"And they've been drinking too much."

Allyson shook her head. "When we've fixed the education crisis. We'll take on alcohol."

"Ready, Chief."

Chapter Twenty-Two

"Drew's done a helluva job, Allyson. I wonder if we shouldn't give him some more time for interviews and research so he can turn this into a series."

"He's very sharp, Jeff, and very intuitive. He knows where to look and where to follow up. I'll ask him but I'm pretty sure he could line up a half-dozen interviews to expand what he already has."

"Any new angles?"

"Oh, yes, I'm sure."

"There's one he might check out down here. Over in Jersey. Mahwah. My wife heard about it at her book club. They have a weekly called the *Mahwah Register* and one of their reporters did a piece about a local group putting a measure before the state legislature that would support the right of girls to get an abortion without getting a parent's permission. I looked it up. A fairly balanced piece. She reported that the local school board opposed the measure.

"It turns out that the wife of the *Register*'s publisher was on the school board, and she was furious that the story was in the paper. She got her husband to fire the woman."

"You're kidding. And he did?"

"Yes. But you might have Drew look into that, too, as an example of how the school boards can exert social power in a community. Granted this is an unusual situation, but there's plenty of cross-pollination in small communities, and not a lot of opportunities to spread out the responsibilities."

"I will tell him."

"Oh, and there's another angle that is probably worth some ink, and that is poor teachers. I know most of our coverage is about how they are caught in the middle, between the authorities and the parents, which no doubt is from where most of the problems arise, but bad teachers have a particularly significant role in leaving children poorly educated, or worse. Discouraged from learning or getting on their proper life track. We talked about remembering the great teachers in our lives, maybe have Drew query the other bureaus for stories about teachers who failed their students."

"Very important, Jeff. Especially with all the burn-out, the teachers on drugs."

"I'm thinking of those in the so-called "rubber rooms" here in the city. Some 700 teachers, removed from the classroom for one reason or another – and usually a serious one – and they're there every day in the rubber rooms, all day instead of being fired because it's so difficult to get rid of them. Thanks to their unions."

"It's disgraceful. We all know of the teachers who shouldn't be teaching, some of them just because they're not good at it, and others because they're mean. A friend of ours out in California had a very bright boy who found high school painfully dull. The school had no way to accommodate him. Other schools would let such students sit in the back of the room and read ahead in the textbook, testing with the rest of the class, but otherwise on their own. Not this school.

"The teachers called in the parents and said they thought the boy should be put on Ritilin. The parents were outraged and said absolutely not. So the teachers got back at this boy. He was marvelous in fashioning things with his hands and wanted to take a woodworking course, but instead they put him into a home ec class."

"Yeah, that's the sort of thing we need to expose." Jeff thought for a moment. "I will talk with our digital people about setting up a special feedback line on these reports and see what we get back."

"Yes, good. And by the way, this boy in California, he wound up very angry. He should have gone on to college but didn't. He got a job, but not very satisfying. And then he turned to drugs, and had a number of run-ins with the police. His mother feels guilty about not finding him another school, but they didn't have the money to put him in a private school, and their jobs prevented them from moving so she puts his current problems on the way he was treated at the school."

"She's probably right. Statistics show clearly that young people who run afoul of the law have usually had trouble in school." He swore under his breath. "People don't realize that the children are the clients. They are not in school to provide jobs for the teachers and the administrators."

"I'll pass this all along to Drew, Jeff. And thanks for your support."

"You get the thanks, Allyson. It was your idea, and a very good one. Let me know if you ever want to climb up the executive ladder."

Allyson laughed. "I appreciate that, but I'd rather stay where I am. I love what I do."

Chapter Twenty-Three

It was a Tuesday evening and the scene was an auditorium at a high school in a Sacramento suburb. The topic was "Teachers and Guns" and it was being sponsored by a local group of NRA members. The program had started with a presentation by them on why it was practical to arm and train teachers in the schools. The moderator then asked if there were any questions or comments. After several seconds, a man walked up from the back of the room to a microphone in the center aisle. He was a young man, probably early thirties, and those who were close enough saw many more years in his eyes.

The man stood at the microphone for a while, looking at the five men and a woman who had delivered the NRA position. Then in an even but strong and penetrating voice, he asked their spokesman who had returned to the podium on the stage, "Have you ever shot a person?"

"No, I haven't had to."

"I have. I've killed five human beings. I was in Afghanistan. On three different occasions, I found myself in situations where if I didn't shoot these people, I or some of the people I was working with, would have been killed."

"Well, we appreciate what our armed forces had to deal

with, sir. Thank you for your service."

"You don't know what you're talking about. I am a doctor, pledged to saving lives, not taking them. I was in Kandahar working in a clinic, trying to save the lives of civilians being systematically threatened and tortured by the Taliban. Three times they came into my clinic, once to finish off a young woman who had been stabbed trying to escape her family. Once to kill a young man who had been beaten nearly to death for teaching at a local school...in front of his students. And the third time, two men came after me with assault weapons they'd bought from the local police who'd gotten them from American forces, to kill me for the work I was doing trying to save lives."

He cleared his throat and changed direction. "Have you taken a safety course, required if you apply for a concealed weapons permit in California? They tell you the difference between shooting hot and cold. Touch your ear lobe. If it's hot you are probably angry. Angry is a dangerous emotion to have when you are thinking about shooting a gun, especially at someone. You're not very stable. Your aim is questionable at best. Your ability to make rational decisions is in the toilet. The same, sometimes worse, if you are afraid. You have all the problems of being angry, plus you feel threatened, and there's a desperate and growing sense of urgency."

The doctor paused. "And all that's true when you know how to shoot. When you're familiar with guns, know how to handle them, can tell if your weapon is loaded just by the feel. You know – not think but know – there's a bullet in the chamber. You're ready to squeeze the trigger not jerk it. You are aware of what is behind your target in case you miss or your bullet goes through him."

The Bright Wise Solution

He shook his head. "So you're a teacher and suddenly someone bursts into your classroom with an AR-15. First you're going to need to unlock your desk drawer, if you can find the key, if your hands aren't shaking so much you can get the key in the lock. Then you're going to have to put bullets in the gun because they wouldn't want you to keep a loaded gun in your desk. Okay, ready? It's not like you're at a firing range, if you've ever even been, looking down your private lane with a full-front, stock-still target at the other end. You won't have headphones to reduce the noise, and instead there will be thirty children jumping around screaming. That should help focus your aim. But before you fire, make sure the area around and behind your target is clear in case your shots go wild, or the target moves, or your bullets go through him."

He stood there shaking his head slowly. "How do you think such a plan would have worked at Parkland or Sandy Hook? Think about the shooting in Maryland where the officer fired his gun at the killer but missed; it turned out the killer shot himself. Or think about the teacher in California who was a cop and safety officer who fired a shot into the ceiling mishandling his gun, which shouldn't even have been loaded. Or the Parkland chemistry teacher who somehow left his Glock 9mm on a bench in a public restroom and when he went back for it, found a homeless guy holding it and who fired off a shot before he got the gun away from him.

"And you tell me that America is going to train its teachers to such incredible levels that they will be able to handle a madman with an assault weapon walking down the hallway of their school? This when even the cops are stymied; remember there was one armed officer

The Bright Wise Solution

who remained outside Parkland when the shooting started. The poor guy. No doubt scared out of his socks. And right to be.

"Did you know that LAPD cops are taught that even if they are pointing their gun at a criminal, the criminal can pull a gun out of his pocket and shoot the cop before the cop can fire? It's true, and why? Because the criminal has made his decision to act, and the cop has yet to decide to fire his gun. It takes only a fraction of a second to make that decision but that's too long.

"Something else you probably didn't know. The historian S.L.A. Marshall wrote that in any given unit of American infantry in combat in the Second World War, no more than one-fifth, and generally as few as 15 percent, had ever fired their weapons at an enemy, indeed ever fired their weapons at all except when first training. Training people to shoot a gun is one thing. Training them to kill is beyond the capability of most people. Putting armed people in schools only invites disaster. Mistaken identification. Someone runs screaming into a classroom with blood on his hands. A victim or a killer? There's a man with a gun...a killer or a plainclothes cop? And we expect our nation's teachers to make these snap decisions?"

He looked at the NRA group. "You people scare me. You are a far greater threat to the safety of our schools than the hypothetical attacker."

The doctor sat down and there was a long silence. Then one person started clapping and then another and another, and soon the entire audience, with the exception of the NRA group, was on their feet applauding. The doctor remained sitting, quiet, stoic. When the applause ended and the audience had regained their seats, one of the moderators asked, "Do you, doctor, or does anyone here, have a suggestion about what we might do to at least stem the violence?"

From amidst the silence, someone in the back of the room, said in a strong voice, "Yes. Turn off the television." A number of calls from around the room agreed. Then the woman who had made the suggestion stood up. "I didn't make the comment lightly. The average American child watches four hours of television a day. That's more time than they spend focused on learning in school. And a great deal of what they see on television is unhealthy, as in twenty acts of violence in an hour of programming. Almost half of all cartoons feature violence. And two-thirds of primetime shows are violent. By age 18, an American youth will have seen 16,000 simulated murders and 200,000 acts of violence."

She continued. "And it's not just television, it's the video games. One I read about – I wouldn't dare watch – showed people invading a sorority, breaking the women's necks and pulling out their spinal cords." There were loud sounds of disgust from around the room. "I won't say any more about the content except that it is depraved and there is a vast number of such hideous programs that are being sold and watched. Some of them are so popular that maybe a million are pre-sold before they are even released.

"The fact is that people can't watch, let alone play, these awful games without them having some effect. Most common is it desensitizes them to violence in general, and especially toward women, because they are designed to legitimize misogyny. People playing these games are essentially anti-social. In their defense, most of the parents of the children who play these games have no idea how grotesque these games are, but very frequently, the parents are the ones making the purchases, pressured by their children, wanting their children's love or approval.

"And let me add that much of the music the young people are listening to also celebrates violence, and the listeners are affected by it. Studies have shown that rap and hip-hop listeners are more apt to drink alcohol, do drugs, and act violently."

"So do we ban video games and rap music?" someone asked from the other side of the room.

"I wouldn't suggest it," she responded, "as it would probably add to the appeal, especially for younger people. As with the video games and the television and movies that promote violence and hatred. No, the problem isn't with the children..." She let that sit for a good five seconds, and then completed her thought. "The problem is with their parents for failing to provide them with a functional moral compass."

"Who are you, lady, to tell people how to raise their kids?"

The woman looked at the person who had angrily questioned her. And then she said, "I wonder that you would ask. It doesn't matter who I am. It's the information that is important. The evidence is clear that violent entertainment produces damaged, dangerous people. Why should parents want to allow, let alone abet it? And I'll go farther. I believe that if we are to succeed, the community needs to support the parents. It truly does take a village to raise a child. Not nosy, prying neighbors, but good people who are making an effort for the next generation to have a healthy and productive future.

The Bright Wise Solution

Is that wrong? Do I have better credentials if I tell you that my college roommate still hasn't gotten over the loss of her daughter at Sandy Hook?"

Chapter Twenty-Four

"Look what I found" said the subject line in an email Drew sent to Allyson. She clicked the link and it took her to a page titled "A Failing Grade" by Murray Aaron Stone.

"I know that name," she said aloud, and then tried to remember from where. After a few moments, as she started to read what appeared to be an essay, she gave up trying to remember as she was engrossed in the text.

Save Our Schools

We spend a trillion dollars a year on things military, and yet our nation doesn't feel very secure. There are a number of reasons, including that our military is led by people preparing to fight the last war. And there are our representatives in Congress, of both parties, who say yes to every military bill for fear of not preserving national security, in the meantime, bankrupting our nation of the funds needed for rebuilding our infrastructure, providing health care, feeding hungry children, and revitalizing our public schools system.

The fact is that we don't need more missiles and tanks; we don't need to have our soldiers in 149 foreign countries.

What we need is to come together again as a nation. To restore the meaning of "United" to a divided and polarized society.

We are at odds with each other – rich and poor, black and white, young and old. We divide along religious and political lines. In truth, we are a very angry people, and are struggling with great fears. And at the core of all of these divisions is our ignorance.

I get conflicted sometimes because I see the United States as the historic synthesis of the Eastern spirit and the Western intellect, and we should be the shining city on the hill. But we have been destructively dumbed down, both in intelligence and decency. I don't know how, or if we can, recover. At least not without some sort of global disaster that forces us back on ourselves, and then puts us demonstratively dependent on intellect and integrity. I do know that we must do a totally better job of educating the succeeding generations to the values of intellect, consciousness, and truth if we are to have any hope for life's future on this planet of ours.

Do you disagree? Consider that at the time the United States was invading Iraq in 2003, two-thirds of Americans surveyed could not find Iraq on a world map, although they could name all of the judges on "American Idol." Or when a few years ago, in random interviews with students on a university campus, most couldn't name the vice president of the United States, or even say who had won the Civil War. But they all knew who was the husband of Angelina Jolie.

The Bright Wise Solution

One of the reasons why Americans have become out of touch with their critical citizen duties is the migration from reading the printed word to the electronic alternatives. They get their news from television, the internet, often misleading fake news passed along from friends and associates. They spend far less time becoming accurately informed, and even less having any real sense of what is going on in their government and society, choosing instead to tap sources that tell them what they want to hear, or that simply provide them with what they find entertaining. Their attention span for important information has shrunk to useless dimensions. Grievously, they have stopped reading, not only newspapers but also books.

Consider these statistics:

– Fewer than 50% of U.S. adults are able to read an 8th grade level book.

– Half of college students will never read another book after they graduate.

– Fewer than 20% of U.S. families bought a book last year.

– Fewer than 15% of U.S. prison inmates can read and write.

We are not only ignorant, but it appears to not bother us. In the early 1980s, a joke circulated about a survey in which people were told that Americans seemed uninformed and apathetic and asked what they thought about it. The common reply was, "I don't know and I don't care." But this is not a joke. Ignorance and apathy threaten the very foundations of our democracy. Thomas Jefferson put it succinctly more than two centuries ago when he said, "If a nation expects to be ignorant and free, in a state of civilization, it expects what never was and never will be."

Compounding our crisis situation today is the larger problem that we are not doing anything about it. It would take something on the order of a *deus ex machina* intervention for the American citizenry to awaken to the immediate need for intelligent leadership, enough so that they would do their informed duty at the polls. And as that would require a literal miracle, there is a need to look for another solution.

While it is possible that a once-in-a-century leader – a combination of the Roosevelts, Lincoln, Kennedy, and our Founding Fathers...and probably a woman – will surface, our only option seems to be to upgrade the electorate. Moving most expeditiously, presuming that eight-year-olds are educable, it would still take us ten years to develop a voter movement that could deliver us a new Congress and put a top-quality president in the White House.

These will have to be remarkable leaders because as of this writing, several months before the 2018 midterm elections, tremendous damage has already been done, and a great deal more will be ruined simply in the neglect of the existing crises in the economy, health care, infrastructure, justice, and, of our greatest threat, the environment. That noted, these crises, especially the rapidly-deteriorating global environment, will make a stronger case for the need for dramatic change.

But how is that change to be effected? It must be done through education, of course, which means schools, plus efforts outside of the existing public schools system. In order to map out the future, it is necessary to answer four questions:

> – Where are we? which requires a clear, accurate definition of our current state;
>
> – How did we get here? so that we know the routes we took, the reasons why, and the people and organizations that led us to where we are;
>
> – Where do we want to go? because we need to define and describe in reasonable detail what (semi-) perfection would look like and shoot for it; and
>
> – How do we get there? which means how do we leave where we are and get to where we want to go, always willing to alter our course as appropriate.

So first, understand where we are. Our education system is about preparing the next generation to assume roles to function in our capitalist society; to "earn" their living in support of the economy. It is not about seeing who the children are and who they might become. It is not about opening their minds. It is not about tapping into their inherent capabilities. It is not about sparking or finding venues for their creative instincts, to satisfy the hunger in their souls. It is not about discovering the contributions they might make to a healthy society.

What we should be offering children, from their earliest social age is a smorgasbord of opportunities, exposing them to different ideas, creative endeavors, and a wide variety of puzzles and paints and games, to see what might catch their interests and illuminate their proclivities.

Second, how did we get here? There have been stellar times in our history. Think of the intellectual and spiritual greatness of our founding fathers; of Emerson, Thoreau, Webster, Mann, and Holbrook in the early 19th Century; and the rise of intellectualism in the early 20th Century when schooling became accessible to millions of American children through the iconic one-room schoolhouses. But in the post-World War II era, the quality of public schools began a significant decline. Whereas before the war, education was valued. After the war, America went to a new phase of growth and wealth. And in that time, the pursuit of education took on a different texture. Going to school was important because the children wanted to grow up and get a good job, though that didn't always mean college.

The larger point is that education was not about expanding the mind, it was about getting ahead. And not only was the purpose altered, but the role of state and local school authorities grew with the purpose of tailoring the curriculum to their own social values. This continued a pattern of strengthening the role of religion in defining what the children would learn, particularly in downgrading the value of science, and in such critical areas as evolution, which was simply not taught in many of the more backward areas, especially in the South and parts of the Midwest.

Schooling slacked off in many important subjects, and the decline of the education process was furthered by wholesale social changes in the Sixties. There were seven revolutions in that decade and all affected our schools.

– The anti-war movement which was of particular

interest to young men who faced the draft.

– The civil rights movement, which enfranchised blacks, upending the long-accepted social structure, especially in the South.

– The women's liberation movement which enfranchised the larger half of the population, and dramatically increased competition in the workplace.

– The sexual revolution which, with the birth control pill, turned social mores upside down.

– The consumer revolution which took power from the makers and gave it to the buyers.

– The environmental movement, sparked by Rachel Carson's *The Silent Spring*, which dramatically raised consciousness about our lapsed stewardship of Spaceship Earth.

– The communications revolution with television assuming an enormous role in the lives of American families.

Today, the television is on an average of five hours a day in the average home, and seven hours a day in the homes of some of the people living at the lower end of the financial spectrum. Compounded with the massive use of smartphones and the internet – plus the inordinate loading of homework on children from the earliest grades – the possibility of experiencing a quality education has disappeared for but a few.

Each of these revolutions might have caused a major upheaval in any society, but in our country the changes were absorbed far more smoothly than might have been predicted. At least on the surface. In truth, looking back, there are claims that the new sexual freedom and empowerment of women fractured the family unit, and these claims were not without some merit. With women entering the workplace, marriage patterns changed, and parenting suffered some serious cutbacks; remember the term "latchkey kids"? There was also a significant diminution in the role of fathers, destructively so, and the responsibilities of the mother also changed in important ways. Both parents were diverted to some extent from providing the guidance to their children that had been the previous norm. The children lacked the attention and the training in social skills, and what it meant to be a grown-up in today's world.

Not all parents dropped out. Many of the religious fundamentalists saw the social changes as a threat to their way of life and recognized that schools were a practical venue to protect their interests. They organized and exercised political clout to force publishers to produce textbooks that reinforced their reactionary views on religion, history, and life. Activists in large states like Texas could have an effect on other states because the publishers eschewed the idea of rewriting and editing for school districts with less buying power.

Viewing the religious campaigns as coming from the right, from the left came pressure to implement – or at least try – a variety of new concepts in teaching, many of them far from what the teachers had been practicing for decades and longer. Yes, there were certainly areas that needed updating and refining as the world had changed, and understanding and preparing to function in the "new" world required more and different information. But many of the babies (and older children) wound up being washed out with the bath water.

And not only on the pedagogical front but in societalization as well. Discipline broke down in many schools where authorities decided that more permissiveness was essential in order to give more children more room to grow themselves. Compounding this approach were federal programs like "No Child Left Behind" that invariably lowered the bar that all students had to reach, both in academics and behavior. This not only caused tremendous damage to the once-vaunted American public schools, driving the test scores of American children to the bottom rungs among developed countries. These "innovations" also made teaching an impossible task.

Where all this left the nation's public schools was in a declining maelstrom of failure and despair.

The answer to question three, Where do we want to go begins with reprising the purpose of schools, which, simply put, is to prepare the next generations to become functioning members in society. Most people think that means academics that will imbue the students with the know-how to get jobs and learn enough about society to properly manage their role in it. But the fact is that schools have to pick up the ball many parents have dropped, and that is to make the children into healthy, thoughtful, moral, honest, competent, constructive, intellectual, curious, conscious human beings. Yes, that goes against the grain for a sizeable majority of parents, but the proof is in the disastrous results generated by that majority.

Okay, and finally question four, How do we get there from here? Yes, this is an enormous undertaking, but if

The Bright Wise Solution

the parents haven't done it, and the schools don't do it, who will? Their peers? Social media? The police?

This daunting task, which would be far more manageable if the parents did their part, and properly, is doable, but it requires the finest quality teachers society has ever imagined; people of character with great minds who are committed to this challenge in a way most teachers today couldn't even fathom. But if they did understand the importance of first-rate teachers – if that's why they signed up for these low-paying, often thankless jobs – then they should be at the top of the list for consideration as new teachers.

These new teachers need to be able to identify the proclivities of their charges, to put before them the opportunities that are best suited to their interests and skills. They must be able to ignite the spark of curiosity that will grow the child into the kind of person that best fits his natural abilities and personality.

This is such an important role that it must be recognized, celebrated, and properly rewarded. Teachers who have the skills to identify the needs of students and to help them grow to the best they can be – for themselves and for society – are true heroes. Just imagine who might become teachers if they were paid the kind of salaries that are lavished on football players. Currently the average starting salary for a teacher is $70,000 while the rookie football player is paid $795,000.

Of course we're not going to find the full contingent of teachers of this quality to fill all the openings in all of the schools, not right away. But considering the value the students of these teachers will have to offer down the road – as teachers themselves, for example – we must focus the talents of the gifted teachers on the gifted students – those who are most likely to be ready to carry the baton on the next cycle.

As much as we might think of leveling the proverbial playing field for every student, regardless of potential, we don't have that luxury at this time. We may never have such a bench of great teachers to meet the needs of every student, but certainly not now. And we would not be the first country to select the best students according to their skills, and our needs. We need to best deal with the existing crisis for the benefit of society in the near term, as failing to exercise that discretion could, as it already threatens today, mean that there won't be a long term.

Don't feel threatened or frightened. We've gotten this far against great odds. We have a pathway to resolving the problems that face us today with sharp minds, dedication, and collaboration. It is encouraging when you think back on your time in school, about the great teachers who gave you faith in yourself and the educational process. If you are like most people, you can likely remember perhaps five such standout teachers. I am grateful to this day for

- Miss Deinlein who taught fourth grade, and seated us with the brightest students in the back of the room so she could better serve the slower students in the front;

- Miss Doolittle who taught eighth grade social studies. She'd been a sergeant in the First World War and was very serious about her students learning about history and geography;

– Chuck Trout taught history in my senior year in prep school and also organized students to go out into the community to raise support for the Housing Rights Act before Congress that spring;

– Rose Soffer taught theater at a college summer school program and drove us around the region to see summer stock theater featuring such stars as Frank Langella, Stacey Keach, and Anne Bancroft; and

– Professor Richard Harrier taught Shakespeare during my first year in college with such a love of the work that he would start reading aloud from the book, and then slowly the book would come down and he was reciting from memory.

But most I remember Robert Moriarty, who was the principal of my elementary school. One morning, he came into Miss Finn's fifth grade class and brought me out to his office. There he and I spent the whole day going through new math textbooks that had arrived for his edification. We read about universes and different number-base systems, including the *gobo*, which was base five, and more that I don't remember. But that was one of the most special moments in my life. What I learned that day in 1961 from this very good man was a benefit a decade later when I was learning binary computer programming in college. More to the point, I saw what it meant to learn one-on-one with someone whose only purpose was to share the excitement of discovery.

Private schools have been leading this charge but have been under attack for not taking all comers, not only those who can't afford the fees but those who aren't performing at a higher level. Or who have obvious impediments to learning. It is important that the likely new leaders be given the best education possible, without teachers being distracted by those children who aren't ready to ascend to critical thinking and leadership roles.

I would also encourage the alums of the finer prep schools to press the administration of their schools to focus on developing the students for service to the nation, to look to finding roles in rebuilding our nation with the qualities our founders sought to imbue. Instead of breeding young corporate CEOs or Wall Street attorneys, let them provide the impetus for these people to take positions where they can restore our greatness and take us to a new level. We need quarterbacks now, not linemen.

* * * * *

"Who is this guy?" Allyson asked Drew that afternoon, stopping by his desk when she had finished reading the piece.

"I didn't know either and I looked him up. It's a *nom de plume* of a retired network news producer. He's been out of the biz for decades, but he's written a lot. Mostly novels, it turns out, but he's kept his hand in with the journalism. He emails out a lot of articles a day to a small list of people who appreciate his discernment when it comes to being informed."

"Have you spoken with him?" Allyson asked.

"No, I wanted to wait until you decided what you wanted to do, if anything, about him."

"Talk to him. Find out why he wrote the piece, who saw

it, does he expect anyone to take action on what he's written. There are a lot of people out there who would no doubt agree with it and be interested in supporting the direction he is supporting. Also, ask him who he thinks might be interested in his approach."

"On it, Chief."

She laughed. "Very brave of you."

Chapter Twenty-Five

"Mr. Stone?" Drew asked to the curt "yes" he received when his call was picked up.

"Yes, again," the voice replied. Then he said, "Mr. Ekland, isn't it? With the *New York Tribune*? I'm not surprised that you called. I've read your pieces on schools. Very substantial."

"Why thank you, Mr. Stone," he said, and then added, "That means a lot, coming from someone with your experience."

"Yeah, I've got some cred. What can I do for you, sir?"

"Your essay 'Save Our Schools' was most comprehensive, and the direction you laid out made eminent sense. I wonder if you'd gotten any traction with it."

"You mean from funders?"

"Yes, funders, but also consultants, school reform organizations, educational firms…"

"Let's cut to the chase, may we? You want to know if my idea is going to get off the ground."

"Yes, sir."

"There was considerable response, mostly negative from the do-gooders and the teachers' unions, as you might expect. The former wants everyone to have everything – the t-ball crowd who thinks nobody should strike out – and the teachers' reps who are worried shitless that they'll lose membership and dues revenues because their members will face quality competition they won't be able to match.

"But there was also less but more significant response from parents who wanted to sign up their little Jack and Jill. Some people at the top colleges – off the record, at least for the moment, as you might imagine – are very excited that they could be served up quality students. And the bottom line about the bottom line is that I heard from serious money folks who wanted to know what kind of numbers I was talking about."

Drew asked, "Was that what you expected?"

"Actually it was. I ignored the complainers – mostly parents and self-styled liberals who thought I was trying to end the world as they know it, which I suppose I am. And I didn't take seriously most of the teachers who responded, because those who have the smarts and the skills to get with the program are going to do very well when the time comes. And they know it will take some time to get rolling, while those who lack what's needed are going to play second fiddle in the minors, if you'll pardon the mixing of my metaphors.

"I got a number of emails and calls from some of the quality folks in the charter business – the people who are running the top-rated schools today – who said they were excited about what I had said and looked forward to talking to me when it was appropriate."

There was a pause that sounded like Stone was taking a drink of something. "Sorry, I needed some more caffeine.

Anyway, the big question of money got some very strong answers. I was delighted, of course, because it turns out there are a lot of people out there with ten figures to spend on an educational system that will work, and they contacted me because they realized that what I was talking about will."

"That is wonderful news, sir."

"I thought so. Thanks. I told them that I was a journalist, which of course they knew, and that I would make no pretense at setting up a company, let alone an enterprise of the size and scope that my ideas would entail. But that shouldn't be a problem. In fact, more than one of these money folks told me how refreshing it was to talk to someone who didn't want to run the show. They also said they could recommend people who do that sort of organizational design and development and that I would have the option to pick those I wanted to work with."

"More good news."

"That was my take. Listen, Mr. Ekland, we have more to talk about certainly. Give me your email address. I have your phone number, and I'll get back to you sooner than later, when I have a story for you. Right?"

"That's great, thank you. I wonder, sir, if we might get together face to face, sooner than later. I think this is going to be a long and interesting journey, and it would be most valuable to me if we might meet."

"Yeah, all right. I'll get in touch with you."

Drew gave him his email address, and said good-bye. When he got off the phone, he sat back and took a deep breath. When he let it out, he offered this comment to the ethers: "Holy shit."

Chapter Twenty-Six

"Allyson, this guy's for real. He's got some serious people interested, including big money. And he's got some serious people upset with him."

"You're right. Both important signs. What's next?"

"He lives in Carmel – not Indiana, Carmel-by-the-Sea on the Monterey Peninsula – but he's coming east next week, to Washington, at the behest of the Equal Education Alliance. They want to try to change his mind. Good luck to them. I'm going to shuttle down to D.C. and have a meal with him. He's very pleased that the *Tribune* is on this story."

"What sort of 'behest' is it?"

"A panel on the future of education but judging from the participants, it looks like they're looking at Stone as more of a target than a contributor since the other three people on the panel seem to share the Alliance's politics."

"Will you be there?"

"Yes. The press release Stone sent me said it was open to the media."

"Aarrgghh."

"I know you hate that term, Allyson, at least as it is applied to us, but they, like so many others, are only interested in favorable coverage."

"Have we given them any ink in the past?"

"I checked. We noted in passing that one of their execs testified at a House sub-sub-committee on federal funding of religious schools, but we didn't say what she said, just that she was invited to testify."

"You're smart to get close to him, Drew. The better he knows you, the more he will trust you."

"That's been happening already. I even asked him why he used the pseudonym. He said because there are too many crazies out there, and not just the social ranters, but real crazies who think they hear god and god – their god – wouldn't like what Stone says."

"Smart man. There were a number of shootings of doctors who performed abortions. Today, being cautious is smart, not paranoid."

"Did he tell you his real name?"

There was a long moment's pause, and before he answered, Allyson cut in. "Never mind. I don't have to know. You should keep your trust with him."

"Thanks, Chief."

Chapter Twenty-Seven

The fact that the Equal Education Alliance had chosen to have their panel discussion on "Equal Rights, Equal Schools" at the Holiday Inn in neighboring Arlington, Virginia, Drew surmised, was probably an indication of their tight budget. The space was, he estimated, about 2,500 square feet, and with the two tables and five chairs in front, the room was comfortably filled by 100 chairs for the audience. Along the back wall, he saw, was a particularly scant offering of pastries that had been cut in half to meet demand, three urns of coffee, decaf, and hot water for tea, Styrofoam cups, and the appropriate accoutrements.

Drew hadn't taken the seven o'clock shuttle for nourishment, at least not for breakfast. From much experience auditing such events, he knew that most of those attending were of the mind that frugality, at least in public, was a display of nobility. Watching the people entering the room, most of them reasonably well-appointed, Drew was of the mind that in private, many of them played their lives more generously.

The meeting opened with the moderator explaining the purpose of the gathering – to search for better ways to assure equal education – and he then introduced the panel. Each of the panel members then said a short bit about themselves, the three supporting the organization's premise citing the years they had been working for equal education for all. Murray Stone was the last to speak. As Drew later described the scene, he could feel the tension in the room rise even before the man started to speak. He could see on Stone's face that he sensed it too.

"There is little more important than education that can help to make this a better world. I've known this from my earliest days in school when I saw that some of the people in the class were there to learn and to grow their minds, and some were not. Some because they lacked the intellect and social skills, and others because their emotional structure positioned them against participating, even though it would be to their benefit that they did. That distinction has been reinforced throughout my life, and has become particularly obvious during the past half-century. I continue to seek ways to change these patterns."

The moderator thanked Stone and then announced to the audience, "We are most pleased to have these distinguished panelists here with us this morning, and since most of you know their work, they agreed that the most efficient exchange of information might come about with their answering your questions. So that's what we will do. Two of our volunteers have wireless microphones and will bring them to you if you'd like to ask a question. You can pose your question to the whole panel or to an individual. Please keep your questions short so that we might get more answers in. Okay? All right, who has a question?"

Drew had positioned himself close to the front at the end of a row so that he could have a good view of the audience. He had noted that when the meeting was called to order, about fifty of the chairs were filled, with people scattered around the room, mostly in small groups or couples. At the moderator's invitation, a half-dozen hands shot up. The two volunteers with the microphones approached the first hands they saw. The moderator pointed to a short, stocky man who, it was quickly discovered, had a squeakily high voice.

"Yes, Mr. Stone, why do you use a pseudonym? Is it to hide from your racist positions?"

Stone was surprised by the attack, but just smiled at the man and shook his head.

The moderator cut in. "Larry, that is hardly a productive approach to gaining equal education. Do you have a serious —"

Stone interrupted in an even tone. "May I answer his question?"

"Er, yes, sure. Go ahead."

"I use a *nom de plume* – that means pen name – in my public work because I find the world today painfully polarized. Instead of having productive discourse and developing a collaborative approach to resolving the critical issues that face us, we take sides, close our ears, and hurl epithets at each other. For the record, I have been involved in the civil rights movement since I was thirteen, when on my own initiative, I collected signatures in support of the Civil Rights Act of 1964 from all of the teachers and administrators in my junior high school.

"But sir, I shouldn't have to provide my credentials to you or anyone else. It is not who I am that matters, it's my ideas. I've thought long and hard about what I think is the right direction to fix our country by fixing our schools. I would be glad to explain how I came to think what I do, why I believe they would work, and how so many significant and powerful people – currently in education and others outside wanting it to work – are getting behind the development of what I have outlined."

He stopped there, but his eyes remained on the man who called him a racist. The room remained silent for a good thirty seconds, until the man handed the microphone back to the volunteer and sat down.

"Yes, Ingrid," the moderator said, nodding to a young woman in a worn coat on the other side of the room.

"So Mr. Stone, you think you've got, like a plan, and I want to know how you're gonna implement it. Like, you don't seem to have any experience."

"I'm a journalist. I write, and people read what I write. I don't know who they are. I've done a little teaching, but not the kind we need. We need teachers who can relate one-on-one with the students, help them to identify their strengths and weaknesses, find out who they are, help them to get on the right path...for them, for each individual, with the support to thrive. That's not my gig. And I don't have the experience to set up what I'm proposing, but those I'm talking with do know the kind of people who can make this happen."

"Okay," said the woman shrugging as she sat down.

The moderator pointed to an older black woman toward the back of the room. "Maizie, you have a question for our panel?"

"It's for Mr. Stone, again," she said, almost apologetically, in a soft, southern accent. "You seem to be running into a whole mess of complaints, and I wonder if you might just tell us a few of the major changes you'd like to see happen in our schools so our children and our grandchildren, can come out smarter and more able to get good jobs and lead good lives."

"Right off the bat, I think it's essential that we teach the children about history, about where we've been and what we've done. So they can be proud of what we got right, and avoid doing again what we got wrong. For instance, I think it's appalling all the people today who don't know that some six million people were murdered during the Holocaust. Six million human beings were shot, gassed, starved, died as guinea pigs of bizarre medical experiments. Why? Mostly because they were Jewish, and others because they were gypsies or Polish or homosexual or political opponents. Six million people; men, women, and children. One can't imagine the horror of a single person or a family forced into the gas chamber, and this happened millions of times. How can we teach our children and not tell them about what our species did to others of our species?

"We have schools that refuse to teach about evolution because the local school board insists on just teaching that the Bible is literally true. Students don't learn about climate change because local officials insist that it is a hoax. Teachers don't tell students about Martin Luther King Jr. because they are afraid that it might upset some of them. We need to tell the truth.

"We need to make it exciting to learn about life, about who we are, about who the students can become. Schools need to pick up where the parents left off – or maybe they did nothing to prepare their children for school – so that society will have bright healthy minds instead of people who can't or won't act responsibly."

He paused. "I'm sorry, I don't think I directly answered your question. I tend to get on my soapbox when it comes to this subject."

"You sounded good to me, Mr. Stone."

"Well thank you, madam. Here's are specific suggestions. We should expand our school year from 180 to 220 days, the way they do in Europe and Japan. We need ESL programs 24/7 wherever the population calls for them. We need a strong vocational training system nationwide, tied in with regional and national enterprises. We need to prod colleges to start new programs that specifically prepare high school graduates to step into the role of adult members of our society by making sure that they understand what it means to stand on their own. I refer to it as an advanced course in home ec that makes young people more functional in the real world, so they can protect themselves from liars and cheats, and contribute to a stronger, more unified community."

"Bravo to that, Mr. Stone. Too many young people today don't know about credit cards, they don't know about banks. Mostly they know how to spend but they don't know how to save."

"Amen to that, ma'am," Stone said, clapping his hands together several times. The woman sat down. Silence again ensued.

"Yes, sir," said the moderator, nodding to a well-dressed older gentleman a couple of rows in front of Drew.

"Thank you, Harold, for staging this forum. Thank you

also to your panel members, and," he said turning to face the rest of the audience, "thank you all for showing support for quality education." He turned back toward the front.

"I must confess that I didn't come here with an open mind, but it has been opened by what I've heard from Mr. Stone, and I'd like to ask you, sir, a question which may or may not relate directly to the issue for which we came here this morning."

Stone opened his hands in front of him.

"Thank you." He smiled. "I have seen the K-12 term over the years and just the other day, I looked at it and wondered if that perspective should stand. Perhaps it is out of date. It seems very cumbersome to me, considering the vast differences there are between a five-year-old in kindergarten, and a seventeen-year-old junior who drives a car, is boggled by hormones, and is considering life after high school. What do you think about breaking down that K-12 barrier?"

"I think it's a great idea. Someone suggested to me that we shouldn't have grades at all, that we should be far more flexible about moving children ahead to where they are challenged, where they can explore new fields, and find the path that best suits them. The notion that education takes place according to textbooks and a nine-month calendar established to match harvest time is ridiculously anachronistic."

"Indeed, sir. Thank you."

"Thank you, sir," Stone replied. "For raising what is certainly a very important point."

Maybe a dozen other people in the audience had questions or comments, all focused on what Stone had said, and he engaged them all in a gracious and thoughtful manner. Then the small man with the shrill voice was standing again and would have been called on next but the moderator, in his wisdom, looked out at the whole audience and announced that he thought this would be a good place to stop. "A lot of important ideas have been brought up, and I think, to the great credit of those here, some minds have been opened, if not changed. This is what education is all about, and I thank you again for your participation."

With that people started rising and leaving their seats. A number of them came over to speak to the panel, and it was certainly no surprise from Drew's perspective that most of them approached Murray Stone. He moved in their direction and observed from outside as Stone listened carefully and returned with succinct answers to their questions. Between one volley, he caught Drew's eyes and without saying or even showing anything to those from the surrounding audience acknowledged him. After a few minutes, the moderator, who had been talking to – and likely mollifying – the other panelists but keeping an eye on the crowd around Stone, came over to provide the speaker with an exit.

"I don't mean to cut off your conversations, but Mr. Stone has a long flight to get home tonight and we need to let him go."

The half-dozen people around him gave Stone a final round of thanks and dispersed. Drew stayed back as the moderator shook Stone's hand and said his own good-bye, clearly pleased with how the morning had gone. With that, they parted, the panelist joined the journalist and they walked toward the exit.

"Drew, I'm glad you were able to make it down for this session. I think you got a sense of what some of the supposed opposition is about."

"Yes, but also how hungry, as this group was, to hear your ideas. That was the biggest take-away for me."

Stone smiled and nodded his head. They headed out of the building. "Do you have a car?" he asked.

"No, I cabbed it up from the airport."

"I have a car," he said, pointing across the parking lot. "I checked out of my hotel across the river, and my flight doesn't leave until this afternoon. Let's find a place where we can enjoy a long lunch. Then I can drive you back to National."

Drew looked at him questioningly. "I'm flying out of Reagan."

Stone laughed. "Yes, it used to be called Washington National but they changed it to Reagan because he broke the air traffic controllers' strike. I refuse to use the new name unless I have to."

"I like that," Drew said. "Do you have a place in mind to eat? If not, I can recommend a good seafood place, although living where you do, you may want something different."

"Good seafood sounds good. Very healthy, too. Where is it?"

"Right near the airport. I've been there a number of times, and the food has always been good."

"Lead the way, my friend."

Chapter Twenty-Eight

"How was Stone?" Allyson Whyte asked, standing by Drew Ekland's desk.

"Good morning, Chief," he said with a big smile. "He was great. Completely disarmed one guy who went after him, and at the end of the program, he was surrounded by people who wanted to ask him more questions, and thank him for what he had to say."

"Impressive," she responded with raised eyebrows. "What's next?"

"I'm finishing writing up my notes on yesterday with Stone, and then I need to make a couple of calls to people he thought I should talk to. We're getting close to a putting out a big story, I think."

She patted him on the shoulder. "Very good, Drew. I know New York will be happy to hear it. Do you need any help from me at this point?"

He shook his head. "But thanks." She started to walk away, and he said. "Um, maybe..." he stopped a moment. "No, I was thinking maybe of having other people do some interviews with some of the other players so it's not all ours. Give people a sense of how big this is by using other reporters. Let me get back to you."

"Good. You're thinking like an editor. Let me know what

you need."

"Will do, Allyson. Thanks."

She nodded and left him alone, and he went back to his typing. After about fifteen minutes, he shuffled through his notebook, making sure he'd transferred all he wanted into his computer. Satisfied, he saved his file. He picked up his cellphone and copied several names and numbers in it onto a pad on his desk. Then he made his first call to Efram Marx, a litigator in Seattle.

"Mr. Marx, my name is Drew Ekland. I'm with the *Tribune*. Murray Stone gave me your name and number. I'm working on a story about education, and he said your wife has launched a new program, especially targeting children who are being home schooled."

"Yes, Mr. Ekland, Murray, ahem – he's an old and dear friend – sent me a note saying you might call and telling me to cooperate with you." He chuckled. "Yes, my darling wife, Anabel, is wonderful. She was a teacher for 27 years, and when there was an ugly kerfuffle at her school, I ironed it out – got the two miscreants who had tried to frame her fired – and now she is free. But you don't need to know that part. What you want to hear about is what she is doing with her freedom."

"Yessir."

"Don't call me 'sir,'" he said sternly. "It makes me feel old." More chuckling. "Anyway, Anabel and a close former teacher friend decided to put together a program to teach home-schooled children about important historic and cultural subjects that they wouldn't have gotten at home. They wouldn't have gotten them in school, for that matter, but they're still so important to producing a well-informed grown-up."

The Bright Wise Solution

"Interesting."

"Yes, very. So they put together a little curriculum, maybe four classes, and they put out the word to friends. They thought they might get five children to take the classes. They didn't. Inside of two weeks, 48 had signed up."

Drew gave a long whistle.

"Now you're talking," Marx said. "Yes, that was what, eighteen months ago. They had to rent a bigger space and hire three teachers to help them out. They limited the number of students to sixty, and they have a waiting list a mile long."

"Si – Mr. Marx –"

"Call me Efram, Drew. We're going to be good friends."

It was Drew's turn to laugh. "Yes, I feel that."

"Go ahead. I'm a lawyer. I'm paid by the minute."

"What did the parents of these students say about the program, and why they wanted their children to attend?"

"Ah, that's the big one, isn't it? You're good, very good. A mensch. I like that."

"You're padding your bill, counselor. Answer the questions."

"Hah! Okay. They said they knew how important it was for their children not only to learn the facts, but also to understand the context. The more you know about something, the better you can put facts, events, people, situations into perspective. The more well-rounded their children would become with more information."

He paused. Drew was silent. "You got all that? My goodness you are the slowest note-taker I've ever met since Moses was chiseling his tablet."

"No wonder you feel old."

"What? What is that? So anyway, it was also good for these children who had their mother – mostly, sometimes their father – teaching them, to learn from someone who wasn't their parent. Of course. And Anabel and her friend, Joyce, are excellent with teaching children about the world, about life. The children wanted to take all of their classes, and they did. Every one of the children signed up for all the classes with all the teachers."

"How many have come through the program?"

"I think so far there have been over three hundred student classes. That is maybe seventy-five students taking an average of four classes."

"Got it. One more question, if I might."

"Ask away."

"Does your wife want her name and enterprise in the coverage?"

"Of course, what do you think? Stoney gave me your email address. I'll send you information."

"That would be great. I didn't know if they wanted the publicity. What she is doing will have the phone ringing night and day from parents, from other news outlets..."

"From crazy people, especially those lunatic fundies. You know what fundies are?"

Drew laughed. "I suspect you are referring to the holy rollers."

"That's they, yes. And do you know, very curious about the word fundamentalist...curious and appropriate."

"Um, probably not what you're thinking."

"The root of the word is fundament. And if you go look up that word, because I know you won't believe me when I tell you, but you are sitting on your fundament."

"My butt?" asked Drew, surprised.

"You got it."

"Oh my goodness. What irony."

"Irony, maybe, but it explains why the president has so many of the fundamentalists still supporting him despite his terrible behavior."

"Yes indeed."

"All right, sir, and don't feel old. I know you're not. Maybe an old soul. I have a client – a paid client – waiting for me in the lobby. Gotta go."

"Thank you, Efram, my friend."

"Yes, and you too, Drew. Go get 'em.

Drew put the phone down, a smile grew across his face. "He is indeed a mensch."

Chapter Twenty-Nine

The next two calls Drew made were to fellow journalists. The first was to Lisle Brauth, a Swiss writer of international renown whose comments on western world society were frequently printed in the *International Herald Tribune;* no business affiliation, but also of high quality. She was a favorite of very bright, thoughtful people. Clarice Whyte had forwarded a recent Brauth essay on reaching for knowledge and wisdom to her daughter. Allyson had already read it and sent it around to her own "special attn" news list of over 100 friends and colleagues, Drew among them. He had contacted Brauth through her New York agent, asking for a brief interview, and she had set a time that he might call her back.

"Ms. Brauth, Drew Ekland. Good morning. Is this still a good time for you?"

"Hello, M. Ekland. Yes, this is fine."

"I have been an avid reader of your essays, and while I have certainly appreciated your thinking and writing, I can't say that I enjoyed what you had to say. You certainly aren't optimistic about the state of affairs in what we usually refer to as the civilized world."

"I didn't enjoy seeing what I saw, M. Ekland. I think the picture is very bleak. An increasing number of people are deriding the very idea of intellect, of being intelligent, of giving thought to life."

"Why is this so?"

"Of course the simple answer would be the breakdown of our social structure. The changing role of women tore away many of the traditional moorings that once provided a sense of stability. There's the fact that the middle class no longer exists, with some of those people climbing the financial ladder, but most of them being driven down it. Technology has diverted us from conversing with each other. That has left us without understanding of the people, events, and circumstances that affect us. And there is the collapse of our education system, which especially affects the many people on the lower rungs of the social ladder."

"Last month in one of your pieces, you quoted a bit from Susan Jacoby's book *The Age of American Unreason*, writing, 'Local control of schools meant not only that children in the poorest areas of the country would have the worst school facilities and teachers with the worst training but also that the content of education in the most backward areas of the country would be determined by backward people.' That's downright scary."

"It is indeed," Brauth replied, "especially since these backward areas have little input from the outside. Nothing to break the cycle, to rescue those minds with the potential to open and expand.

"And this is a problem across the country, especially in those places where religion dominates, where the attitudes of the populace are anti-intellectual, anti-rational."

"How is that to ever change?"

"I don't know. That book was written ten years ago, and the situation has only worsened. The disaffection of these communities from the elemental principles of America's founding has only grown greater."

"In that book, Jacoby cited some statistics such as two-thirds of Americans don't know what DNA is, and only one in five American adults is convinced that the Earth revolves around the sun. Some might ask why that matters."

There was a short silence at the other end of the line. "I suppose," she began, "that for those who would ask the question, there would be no satisfactory answer. Pedantry is one of the grave problems of our age. There is no humility about ignorance, sometimes there is pride. My view is that not knowing about who we are and the essential truths about life on Earth in the 21st century means that people are not only ill equipped to deal with what we will face from global warming, over-population, and anarchy, but they will advance these crises by lacking the wherewithal to defuse them and supporting those political and other public figures who are furthering them.

"May I add that neither of these points would have the slightest effect on those I'm referring to, except to increase their ire at the author for even offering her views because they would find what she was saying was both confusing and thus, by definition, threatening. It is somewhat ironic that a clearly successful condemnation of their ignorance could be made based on the cost of resources wasted on the vain attempt to educate them."

It was Drew's turn at silence though he kept it short. "Ms. Brauth, as I explained in my first message to you, the *Tribune* is looking to do a major spread on education.

My editor is hoping that you would either write a new piece for it, or have the time for a longer interview."

"I think that would be all right. Why don't you get in touch with me when you know what it is that would work best for your coverage."

"I will do that. And may I close by saying while I am pained by what you have to say, I so very much appreciate that you are saying it. If you only spark constructive thought in a few people, may it be those who will make a difference."

"Thank you, M. Ekland. That has always been my hope."

Chapter Thirty

Another name given to Drew by Stone was Rebecca Costa, a sociobiologist considered by many who have heard her speak or read her books as one of the finest minds of our time. Drew had read a precis of her first bestseller, *The Watchman's Rattle* subtitled *A Radical New Theory of Collapse* but read the whole book before he called her.

In it she wrote about the rise and the fall of three major civilizations – the Mayans, Romans, and Khmer – and how they all followed the same downward path. He highlighted one section near the beginning that read

> "In the beginning, each society overcomes insurmountable obstacles and environmental challenges. They appear to gain control over their surroundings, stabilize food and water, and build systems to assure the safety of their citizenry. Against incredible odds, innovation, diversity, and creativity all thrive. *In these societies, both beliefs and the pursuit of knowledge can be shown to peacefully coexist side by side.*
>
> Then, over time, complexity accelerates and facts become difficult or impossible to acquire. The society becomes unable to solve its problems, particularly those that pose no immediate threat.

Then the society begins passing looming dangers from one generation to the next, as conditions worsen and survival grows more tenuous. Eventually, the society becomes dependent on short-term mitigations and unproven beliefs for remedy. Public policy becomes irrational."

When Drew reached her, he was immediately impressed by how easy Rebecca was to talk with.

"Hi, Drew," she opened, "Murray said you might be calling. Sounds like you're working on something very important. How can I help you?"

"Wow, thank you," Drew managed and took a breath. "At the end of the first chapter of *The Watchman's Rattle*, you summarize what happened to the three major civilizations, their dealing at first with complexity and then later they collapsed. Are we on that track?"

"Ah, yes. Well, Drew, I wrote that book a decade ago and ended that chapter with your question and noted that there's a lot of evidence in our favor."

He could almost hear her wince when she continued. "But now, as was the pattern with the Mayans, Romans, and Khmer, there has been considerable further decline in our political structure, and while I still think we will pull through, I think we will experience remarkable dislocation."

"What has sent us into this spiral?"

"Ignorance would be the simple answer, ignorance based on denial, and both founded by crippling religious beliefs that deny science, refuse to accept facts, ignore real threats. This is what brought down the other societies. They clutched ever more rigidly and tightly to their beliefs in god rather than deal with the reality of circumstances.

"As those civilizations did, so have we had plenty of warning in our situation about over-population, the dumbing down of the citizenry and concomitant rise in fascism, growing pollution and global warming. It's rather astounding that we not only haven't stopped poisoning the land, water, and air, but we continue to do so despite the over-whelming evidence that we literally endanger the continuance of life on Earth. The ocean currents that determine our weather have slowed down; the polar ice is melting. If the Thwaites Glacier in Antarctica collapses, the seas would rise more than two feet, making most of the world's coastal regions uninhabitable.

"But we're in such denial. A columnist in the *Wall Street Journal* had a piece the other day called *The Population Bomb Was a Dud*, dismissing, of course, Paul Ehrlich's book. That's rather incredible since we are, by reasonable estimates, almost six billion over-populated, and increasingly scrounging for clean water and sustenance."

She stopped there, and after a moment, Drew asked her, "What was the evidence in our favor that you saw when you wrote the book?"

"Oh, it's still there. The amazing resilience of our species, the expanded consciousness of many good people, the broadening and focus of our best minds, the hope and energy of the people. Note, too, that we haven't had any quality national leadership for decades, and a true leader might be just what we've been missing to wake us up. Ironically, we may have needed to get into very serious trouble before we would be ready to accept someone or some group to lead us back to a healthy plane.

"But I have to add, Drew, that with my many years of research, and living and working during these fascinating times, I have longed for reaching a point in our evolution where we can pull ourselves up by our proverbial bootstraps." She sighed, "You may be too young to know Tina Turner's *Mad Max* songs, but there was one called *We Don't Need Another Hero*. I would like her to be right, and that we, collectively, become the heroes of our own time."

Drew was quiet. Rebecca came back. "Are you still there? Did you go away because I was talking too much?" she asked in a humorous tone.

"Right here. You are, if I may say, daunting, and in a good way. There's so much power in your thinking, such strength in how you express it."

It took a moment, but she said, "Why thank you. If I may say, that is one of the finest compliments I've ever received. I'm honored."

"I know you travel a lot. If you ever find yourself in our northeast area – Boston, New York, Washington – and are free for dinner, lunch, a cup of coffee, I would be most delighted to meet you."

She laughed, "You're on, Drew. Your contact information is going onto my special list."

Chapter Thirty-One

Drew left a folder of his notes on his phone interviews on Allyson's desk that evening, after she had left for the day. She was in the next morning earlier than he, and when he had had time to settle in at his desk with a cup of coffee, she walked over to talk to him, holding the folder. He had seen her leave her office and recognized the folder she was carrying. He watched her approach, trying to read her reaction, but to no avail. She was a pro and masked her thoughts. But the mask dropped when she arrived.

"You got dynamite," she told him before allowing a smile to show on her face.

"Like it?" he asked, smiling back, unable to hide his pleasure.

"Yes. And I wanted to talk with you before I shared this with New York. First, what's left to bring in?"

"I want to talk to Mur— Mr. Stone – tell him what we have. He knows these people, of course, since he gave me their names and told them I was calling. So there's no question of the integration with his work and their comments."

"My second question is, where is he, and what is his schedule so we know how this might dovetail with what he's doing?"

"I need to update his progress. He was moving fast when we met. I suspect a number of pieces have fallen into place."

"Good, then he may be able to release something significant to us."

"I'll ring him this morning."

"What kind of format are you thinking about? A series? Two-pager?"

Drew showed his surprise. "I, I really hadn't thought about it. I presumed that was your call, and I'm just the typist."

Allyson laughed. "Uh-huh. We can talk about it. I'll need a precis of everything you have, what are the pieces, and how you see them coming together. After you and I go over it all, you can polish it up for Jeff."

"You got it, Chief."

She laughed again. "You know never to say that in front of anyone, don't you?"

"Yes, Chief."

Shaking her head in amusement, she left him to his work. His attention went inward, his eyes peering beyond the horizon. In a few moments, he reached forward and pulled his keyboard toward him. After another long moment, he typed with a creative fury for the next five minutes. Then he stopped, took a deep breath, and pushed the keyboard back to its resting place. "Yes," he said aloud in a quiet and firm voice. Then he picked up the phone and keyed in a number from memory.

Chapter Thirty-Two

Drew was on the phone with Murray Stone for twenty minutes when usually their conversations were an efficient exchange of information that would be concluded in fewer than five minutes. But this time, Stone had a lot of news, and an unexpected starter.

"Drew, I don't need to tell you that you have impressed me, not only with your writing and our discussions, but particularly with your immediate grasp of what I was talking about and what it could mean. Your questions and comments prodded some rethinking and for the better."

There he paused, and Drew thanked him for his generous words.

"That's all well and good, of course," the man continued, "but one of the people who is going to back this effort suggested something that I probably should have thought of first, and that was seeing if you might get the *Tribune* to give you time off to write a book on all of this. After all, you know more about it than anyone else except me, and you've done your own research and writing that flesh out a lot of the issues, small and large, to make it easier for people learning about it fresh to understand the purpose, the plan, and the implementation. What's your first thought?"

"Wow."

"That's a good start."

"I think it would be a great thing to do. Of course, they would want me to have the final say over the content. It couldn't look like a promotional piece."

"Certainly. It would have to be your book, and," he added carefully, "preferably as *Tribune* reporter, although, my friend, if they didn't approve you taking a leave but you still wanted to write it, we would still want you to write it. Of course with no interference from us. A solid, journalistic piece. But I suspect with their going great guns on the subject, they would recognize the value of the association of one of their reporters with what will be a sea change in education."

"Hmm, well I would love to do it, Murray, and I think they would like me to do it. They have a small publishing arm. They might be interested in it that way, too."

There was a slight hesitation on the other end of the line. Stone hadn't considered that angle. "Just so long as you have the final edit, Drew. Not to be difficult but we don't want more cooks at the table. And I trust you implicitly, as a writer, as a journalist, as someone who gets the schools crisis and this program, and based on the facts, not pushing a private agenda."

"I get it. I'll bring it up with Allyson."

There was a sigh of relief at the other end of the call. "Okay, good. Now let me fill you in on where we are. First, three people I've been meeting with over the last couple of months are all in, and when I say all, each is ready to put up 10 figures to start, and assure me that money will not be an object as far as they are concerned.

Second, they have introduced me to several semi-retired executives, all with an understanding of the education crisis and an interest in fixing it quickly, who are ready to put together the infrastructure for this to happen. They know about budgets, acquiring properties, hiring staff, promotion, management...everything."

"Those are a couple of big pieces," Drew remarked.

"Drew, the way the right people – including you – have shown up, it's like the whole thing has been scripted; enter stage left, enter stage right. The people I've met don't need to be persuaded. They are perfect for the areas they were brought in to manage. There will be no stretching of abilities for anyone coming into this project. Everyone has the aptitudes for the specific tasks they've been chosen for."

"That's remarkable, Murray, and a critical aspect of the story."

"I trust you're taking notes," he said with a laugh.

"It wouldn't be otherwise," Drew retorted.

"Good man. Okay, next point. We're looking at opening three centers for sixty students each in different regional markets to make sure we have the kinks worked out before we do a major push. We're looking at starting the classes in mid-August, which will be around the time that the regular school year begins. Backdating the process, we will determine our students at the beginning of May and choose our teachers at the end of March, giving them four months to prep."

"Another wow."

"There are a zillion more details on the structure that is already in an executive summary that I will send to you, but I wanted to give you some of the flavor."

"Delicious."

"We're going to advertise in appropriate venues to retired teachers, good people who quit their current teaching jobs for the right reasons, and mid-lifers with the right skills looking to make the relevant changes. We will also look at young people, thirty-ish, who have the right mindset. We'll be offering them a six-figure salary, resettlement, and three months of training including curriculum development.

"As for finding the students, remembering your conversation with Efram, we expect to be flooded with applications. We will be looking for the children who have a foundation for engaging this program of learning, children who love to learn, who are healthy in mind and heart, and supported – not helicoptered – by their family. We will do some targeted information outreach where appropriate, but we think that press coverage will draw thousands of quality applicants to us through our website. Our promotion will feature real teachers, real parents, and real students explaining the what and why of the program."

"I can see it already. I heard the excitement when I talked with Efram. Murray, I am beyond impressed." Drew chuckled, "I even feel a sense of relief. Like we – the country – have turned a corner."

Stone sighed audibly. "That's where I am, too. And Laurence Selden."

"He's with you? I've never spoken about any names with you."

"He's one of the principals in connecting me to some of

the other key players. He is involved in the design of the schedule and the formulation of the curricula. And of course he will have major input into identification of the likely teachers, many of whom he has met over the years in his consulting. Some have left teaching but would jump at the opportunity to be involved in what we're doing."

"This is so exciting, Murray. What's next for me?"

"I suppose you need to think about the book idea, and if it's a go —"

"It's a go."

" — get clearance from the *Tribune* people to do it. I presume they'll want you to write the story for the news first, which is fine with us. That will make the book an easier task for you. Then I think you'll come out here to meet the other people, not just interview them but get to know them, as they will want to get to know you. If it all goes as I would think it will, the *Tribune* will be happy with the plan, and we can have you out here in ten days."

He paused, and then he asked evenly, though there was anticipation in his voice, "How does that sound to you?"

"It sounds just right. I'm going to get my thoughts straight and then talk to Allyson. She knows how important the story is, and especially the need for what you are doing —"

"What *we* are doing."

"Yes, *we* are doing. She got this ball rolling. She met Laurence Selden. She's dealt with school snafus over her son. I think she'll be fully supportive."

"Good. Another piece to fall into place. All right, my

friend, then I'll let you go. I'll wait to hear from you."

"You won't wait long, my friend."

With that they hung up their phones, one on each coast, and the ball rolled further.

Chapter Thirty-Three

"Got a minute?" Drew stood in the doorway of Allyson's office. She was sitting at her desk, papers spread out before her.

She looked down at the papers and then with a smile at Drew. "Sure."

He walked in, closing the door behind him, and took the chair in front of her desk.

"One of those kind of minutes," she said with a faux frown.

Drew took a deep breath before he started. "It's good news," he began, and then outlined his conversation with Murray Stone, ending with the invitation to chronicle the historic effort with Drew's writing a book.

"Oh, good for you," Allyson said with enthusiasm. "I think that sounds great."

"You do?" Drew was surprised.

"Of course. It's a great opportunity for you, and it will be a wonderful feather in the *Tribune* cap, so to say."

"You think they'll approve my doing it, taking a leave of absence and writing the book."

"More than approve, they'll support you." With that she

picked up the phone and called Jeff Platen. He picked up quickly. "Jeff, you certainly had a great find with Drew Ekland." She listened a moment and then recounted what she'd heard from the young reporter.

"Yes, I have no doubt." She listened again. "Hold a sec, he's right here." She handed the phone to Drew.

"Hello, Mr. Platen."

"We're past that 'mister' stuff, Drew," Jeff said. "This is great news, particularly for you, but also the *Tribune* and, it sounds like, for the country. You must have impressed some very impressive people."

"I think they know what they are doing, Mi – Jeff, and they can make it work. You're right. This could be great for our public schools."

"One question," posed the Editor, "Are you planning to return to work for us? Or do you think you might want to stay with Stone's crowd?"

There was a short silence on the other end. "That was the first issue I considered when I got off the call with him. What would happen if you said I couldn't take the leave of absence to write the book?"

"You thought we would say no?" Jeff interrupted.

"I didn't know."

"Go on."

"My decision would have been to stay with the *Tribune*."

"Good lad."

"And so in answer to your first question, I would want to return here. I'm a journalist, not a chronicler. There are many more important, and just plain interesting, stories to report. And I want to do that for the *Tribune*."

"That's what we want, too. Send me a memo, copying Allyson, of course, tell us when you will leave, and keep us apprised of your progress. Oh, and we will expect you to write the news coverage of all of this, yes?"

"Oh, yes, I would want to do that."

"Of course you should. And I'll talk to the book publishing wing and tell them about what you're doing and to get in touch with you. You probably should get yourself a literary agent to make sure they're offering you the best deal." He laughed at his own words. "Good?"

"Great," Drew said. "And thank you very much."

"You made it happen, Drew. I know you'll make us proud."

Chapter Thirty-Four

Drew was on a flight a week later. Being that the enterprise was organizing around Murray Stone's ideas, and Stone didn't want to – wasn't going to – move from his home in Carmel, they had set up offices in a space on the former Ft. Ord property just north of the Monterey Peninsula. It was next door to the Monterey Bay campus of the California State University, which, it was expected, might serve as a significant resource for input on the curriculum, and a source of new personnel.

Staff people were temporarily put up in new faculty housing that was to be inhabited until the start of the fall semester, nine months away. Drew found himself on the third floor of the former home of a high-ranking Army officer which had been newly remodeled into three separate units, and were fully furnished. His apartment had a living area, a bedroom, a smaller bedroom he would use as an office, a full bath, and a small but well-stocked kitchen. There were even prepared meals in the refrigerator, along with salad fixings and other healthy things to eat. Most appealing was that his top unit had a view of Monterey Bay. As he unpacked his bags, he smiled as he thought about the early winter weather that had blown into New England just after Thanksgiving. Making his escape to the relative warmth of California's Central Coast was a delightful alternative. And the

The Bright Wise Solution

offices were only a verdant half-mile walk away.

The two other housing units in the building were not expected to be inhabited until March, and Drew, having lived in his relatives' house – albeit a large one and they were most gracious about his living there and giving him plenty of space – welcomed the idea of living alone. He could also find his own place to live once he got a feel for his new environs, although he imagined it could be a challenge to find such a comfortable situation as he was moving into. To celebrate his arrival, Drew walked through the neighborhood that had once housed the generals, colonels, and majors, and their families. It was clear from the size of the houses, and the size of the lots, who outranked whom.

What a different world it must have been, Drew thought. Before leaving Boston, he had read up on Ft. Ord. It had been used for maneuvers and artillery training during the First World War. In 1940, the property was converted to a fort and built up. It was decommissioned in 1994 when the Pentagon decided it wasn't worth upgrading and updating during the early BRAC (Base Realignment and Closure) years.

Almost a century, he thought, of training and practicing for war. Now the focus, in their small parcel of the old fort, would be on strengthening the country by producing new generations of bright young Americans ready to grab the reins. "We need to educate people to competence levels in their chosen field of performance," Drew said to himself. He'd been writing the book in his head – and making notes – since Jeff Platen had first okayed the project a week earlier. His mental writing continued, "Enabling them to achieve their dreams – and to love what they do – is the surest route to national security."

It was almost five and approaching sunset; his first in his new digs. He hadn't noticed it before, but there was a bottle of Smith and Hook Cabernet on the kitchen counter with a welcome note from Murray Stone that said, "If you don't like red, I've put a couple of whites in the bottom of the refrigerator." Drew opened the 2016 Bargetto Chardonnay, poured a deep glass, and took it into the living room, sinking into a comfortable leather chair that was already facing the window. He raised his glass to the setting sun, said, "To the program," and then took a long sip.

Chapter Thirty-Five

"What did you think of the program title, Drew?" Murray Stone asked. They were sitting in the Del Monte Café, an unpretentious but attractive little restaurant, on the morning after Drew had moved in. They had just ordered breakfast. The smile on Stone's face spoke only of excitement. "I thought it might be the title of your book, though that's your decision alone."

Before his friend could answer, Stone added, "For the longest time I was working with 'A Failing Grade' but when what I had written, the piece you saw, finally got traction, I realized that it needed a positive title, one that spoke of success rather than failure."

Drew nodded, "Yes, of course."

"And I noodled and noodled about it. I thought about a report card, but that referenced the way we *have* been teaching. It was a way of scoring. I wanted something that was more open, that said both direction and achievement. And as life would have it, I came across something Martin Luther King, Jr. said." He read from his notebook: "'The function of education is to teach one to think intensively and to think critically. Intelligence plus character - that is the goal of true education.' Intelligence plus character is that essential conjoining that we have been missing in leadership, not only in politics but everywhere. Schools, of course, but also science where everyone is working for drug companies or they're competing for a Nobel prize and they don't share critical information. Without character, there is no collaboration."

Drew finally got his chance to answer. "In truth, I hadn't seen the material you had sent me until I was on the plane coming here. I had just slipped it all into a folder. But when I took it out and saw it, I gave the classic long two-tone whistle." He laughed. "I was in an aisle seat, and a very nice-looking flight attendant was just walking up the aisle at that moment. But I hadn't even seen her until she leaned down and said, 'Thank you.'"

They both laughed.

"I like it very much, Murray. Bright Wise really nails it; what we want for the next generation. For them to absorb lots of important information, and become wise with what they absorbed, especially in their fields of interest."

"Yes, that's exactly the way to put it. Well said. But keep it under your hat for the moment, not sharing it with anyone on the outside. Oh, I think it could leak out, but I don't think anyone is tracking us at the moment. I'd like to get all our proverbial ducks in a row before we announce the program." He looked around, whistled quietly, and laughed. "No wonder you're writing our story."

Chapter Thirty-Six

After breakfast, they drove back to the program offices. There Stone brought Drew to the conference room where he introduced him to the six primary managers who would oversee the physical plant, the teachers, the students, finance, administration, and communications. There was an assortment of men and women, of different ages and postures. They knew of his role in the enterprise and eyed him with a mix of curiosity and intention. They all knew what his ongoing coverage in the *Tribune* would mean to their success, especially in the early going.

"Understand," said Stone, "that Drew has full access to what you know and what you're doing. Of course he will respect any confidentiality issues you might have. He's not here to investigate but to understand, who you are, what you're doing, and how you're going about it. After all, this is about who as much as what. I encourage you to ask him for feedback or ideas. Yes, he's writing our story as a titularly outside observer, but he's also intrinsic to our efforts from the inside. I've spent a lot of time with him. You can trust him implicitly."

Drew then told them something of his background, how he had connected with Stone, and the spot-on timing of his move to the New England bureau where he worked

The Bright Wise Solution

for Allyson Whyte who introduced him to Laurence Selden two days later. His connection with the education consultant clearly gave him important credentials with those around the table.

"All right, you'll all get to meet Drew individually so he can get to know you and your areas of expertise, but first I want to show him around our operation, and get him situated. Also, Marty and Joan, I'd like you to sit down with us and go through the preliminary design of the program. He's read the latest iteration, but you might fill in some holes for him." He looked at his watch. "Let's meet back here in a half-hour."

With that he ushered Drew out of the conference room, and gave him a tour of the office space. Like the residential setting, the office space was newly remodeled; in this case, the building had been where the upper level base officers had worked. The rooms were spacious, and Drew was pleased to see, the offices had doors so that people could work in private; not like the one great open space where everyone was visible to everyone else. He could think better without distraction of the sights and sounds of other people. He was also pleased to see a broad array of paper, pads, pens, and other supplies, plus a box of business cards titling him as "Communications Consultant" and listing his new phone number, on his new desk.

"I like this," Drew said to himself. "Very professional, and no skimping." He sat down and noted the comfort of the chair. He went through the drawers, discovering more supplies and an employee phone list. There was also a list, marked confidential, of the principals and officers of the company which included contact information through their chief assistants as well as private cell numbers.

Drew took the stack of folders out of his shoulder bag and laid them on the desk, putting several aside for the meeting he was to have shortly. He checked his watch; still a few minutes before he had to join the others in the conference room. He sat back, closed his eyes, and took several slow deep breaths.

Chapter Thirty-Seven

Marty Benez was the first to come to the conference room, or maybe he had never left. Forty-plus, in an old brown tweed jacket over a white button-down dress shirt, open at the neck, and navy corduroy slacks, the person in charge of hiring the teachers had papers spread on the table in front of him. Drew took a seat across the table from him, and no sooner had he sat down than Murray Stone joined them, sitting at the head of the table. He and Drew chatted about the office set-up for several minutes until Joan Shebat arrived. She chose to sit at the opposite end of the table from Stone. A woman of indeterminate age – Drew would have guessed she was in her forties as well – she presented herself in a manner which said deliberately that her appearance shouldn't matter; scraggily grayish-blond hair, no make-up, and clothes from a consignment shop in Haight Ashbury.

Drew noticed Stone's take on her arrival in a slight flicker of his eyes as she dropped into her chair in a markedly ungracious manner. He also noticed that he himself already disliked her, and that bothered him. He made a deliberate effort to clear his mind of the judgement, with at least temporary success.

"I want to reprise before you," Stone said, looking at

The Bright Wise Solution

Marty and Joan, "what I've told Drew so that if there is anything that needs to be corrected, reinforced, or otherwise adjusted, you can bring it to our attention. But make notes, please, and tell us when I've finished." He turned to Drew.

"Right, the way we have set this up, Drew, and we are always open to tweaking here and there but we think we have a good base structure, is this. First, there is a focus on each student as an individual. We are going to offer him a variety of choices so by exploring them he can deepen his awareness of who he is, what are his true inclinations, and his skills, so that he can choose at least his initial path. Yes, he might change directions later, but he will also – through his looking at different opportunities before he starts out – have a sense of what's out there and what might be another choice." He interrupted himself. "I'm using the masculine pronoun simply because it's easier than using both. In our presentations, we use both or two different examples."

Drew nodded.

"Okay, that said about the individual, the major part of the instruction will be about a national curriculum that will provide the essential foundation for these children becoming full-fledged members of our society. We will instruct them starting with the three Rs, giving them the tools to take in more information. Then we will cover American history in some depth, global affairs, basic science, world religions, economics, the environment, criminal justice, politics....I know I'm leaving off some topics we have on our master list, but you can look at it later.

"This national curriculum has been developed by a team of professors from around the country. They not only have covered a vast number of topics, but they've produced digests of each so that the essentials – facts and nature – can be efficiently taught. They are also providing a layered compendium of more information on each topic so students can explore these subjects further, digging as deep as they might choose. And by the by, we have shown the digests to others in the different fields to make sure that nothing major has been left out of the first level. As you might imagine, the experts in those fields would naturally believe that there should be more of their material in the top digest, and some rewriting has been done, but for the most part, they were pleased with what they saw.

"In addition to the subjective areas, we will also take up psychological and social issues to imbue in our students the ability to better function in personal and group interactions. We will inform them about different character types, and how they take in information differently. Well, you get the idea."

"Pedagogy as well as humanism."

"Exactly. But we're not going to drill down too deeply into any of these topics. We're providing an overview for understanding and competence. As I said, they will also have the opportunity to dig more deeply into any of these subjects that are of particular interest to them."

"That makes so much sense, Murray," Drew agreed. "Most children today have no idea what the various courses of study are that they might pursue, let alone getting even minimal grounding in issues that are important for them to understand as citizens."

"Yes. That's why we are changing the school calendar. Currently, the curricula are designed around a nine-month school year with students taking the same subjects for the full school year. By giving a week's, or a few months', attention to most of these subjects I've mentioned, or longer if they need, we can cover far more ground."

Drew nodded affirmatively. "And there's far less risk of boring students who have no interest in these areas."

"Right. Very important. What was it McLuhan said, 'He who doesn't understand that education and entertainment are inextricably entwined doesn't understand either.' Education has to be interesting for it to have any value."

Stone looked down at a sheet of notes before him. "The watchwords for the program are quality, integrity, and purpose; respect, compassion, and community."

"I like that."

"We also will be providing instruction in what we think of as soft subjects but which will be significant to the students such as home ec, hygiene, nutrition."

"How to open a bank account? Paying off the credit card balance every month?"

"Exactly. I don't know about you," Stone looked around the table, "but my parents didn't tell me about such things and these matters weren't part of my schooling. I had to figure them out for myself, and starting from no outside awareness, I made some needless mistakes."

Marty nodded his familiarity with that learning process. Drew smiled. There was no reaction from Joan.

"Now some structural points. We're going to set up three classes in three cities to start with. The cities are Boston, Minneapolis, and Seattle. The classes will be based on

The Bright Wise Solution

age, the first being for five-year-olds, the second being ten-year-olds and the third being fourteen-year-olds."

"Beginning grammar school, early junior high, and high school levels?"

"Very good, yes. There will be twenty students in each class, two teachers, and two assistant teacher trainees."

"So you're talking about a launch with," Drew quickly calculated, "180 students, 18 teachers and a similar number of teaching assistants. Plus support people, of course."

"Yes. Obviously you've read the outline I sent to you."

"I did, but to hear you describe it, Murray, it comes through ever more clearly. Thank you."

"Good, so I'll run through these other elements quickly and then we can discuss whatever. The Primary class, the youngest students, will be six hours a day, the Central second class will be seven hours, and the Transitional will be eight hours. We had thought of running half-days on Saturday for 40 weeks but opted for these schedules and going for 44 weeks, it breaks down into four quarters of eleven weeks each and with two-week breaks in between.

"Saying it that way, I don't mean to make light of what I think is one of the most powerful aspects of our schedule, and that is that the students can grow at their own pace. Instead of waiting for the new school year to start in September, they can move forward within their class, and ahead to the next class, based on their individual interests and skill levels."

"That is one of the most significant aspects of the program, Murray. Instead of no child left behind, it will be no child held back."

A big smile broke on Stone's face. "When I first came up with the idea, I just sat back and started clapping my hands. I thought back on some of my classes, and there were people in my high school who could have been going to college in the mid to late teens. In this program they would have been better prepared, and hungrier to learn, than having to slog through courses that weren't relevant to them, or were extended for weeks at a time so that the slowest students could catch up." He gave a deep sigh and asked, "Okay, any questions, Drew?"

"I know when I get into this more I'll have a bunch, but for now, I understand the framework and find it exhilarating."

"Good. Marty, Joan what have I left out that you want to bring up?"

Marty looked at Joan who sat looking at Stone but not saying anything, so he said, "I can see why Murray brought you on board. You not only grok this idea but you clearly like it."

Drew nodded his agreement.

Marty asked, "I wonder if you think back on your best teachers, would they have gone along with this?"

"What a good question. And I think I can say unequivocally yes. Of course, not all my teachers by any means. Most would have found the approach threatening; too much change. But the good ones were there to teach, and while they would have wanted to see all of their students getting the best education, they were most interested in moving the best students ahead. Not surprising, of course, since they were the most interesting, the most interested, the more engaging to work with."

Stone looked to Joan. She restlessly shifted her shoulders. In a cranky, somewhat accusing tone, she demanded, "I want to know why you chose him to write our story."

All three men showed surprise at the sharpness of her voice.

Stone, after a moment, replied evenly. "Because he is an excellent journalist, and a fine human being. What is your problem with him?" he asked, his question sounding an edge.

"Well," she huffed, "we're pioneering a sea change in public education and he's led a very pampered life. I looked at his bio and his résumé. What does he know about a hard life, about discrimination? He was born with a silver spoon in his mouth."

Stone looked at the woman for a good ten seconds without speaking, and though she tried to hold the stoicism that followed her charge, it began to break. He waited a little longer before he spoke, and then it was with a sense of reservation. "Is this about cultural appropriation again? I thought you saw the flaws in that position."

She didn't say anything.

"I've come to know Drew, both as a man and as a journalist. I not only have no issues with him as a human being, I hold him in high regard for his work. You owe him an apology."

"An apology isn't necessary, Murray, because it wouldn't be enough. For myself, yes, but not for my grandparents." He took a deep breath and turned to face her. "My grandmother and my grandfather were Jewish and were smuggled out of Nazi Germany when they were only tiny children a few years old. They didn't know anything about what it meant to be Jewish; they were so young. They were hidden in an empty fuel storage tank on a ship that went from Hamburg to Stockholm. They were second cousins and had the same last name, Gerstlein. They were cared for by a childless Swedish couple named Ekland.

"After the war, when they were young adults, they were sent to relatives who lived outside of Minneapolis. From the relatives they found out that their families had died at Sobidor in Poland. My grandparents pretended to be married to have children to keep their two families alive. They had a boy and a girl. The son married a woman who was a teacher in Chicago's South Side. They had me; I was an only child. My father was an engineer who worked for a construction firm that designed highway interchanges so we moved around a bit.

"I didn't learn about my grandparents, who died before I was born, until years later. My father didn't tell me. I found out from my aunt, his sister, who had been told by my grandparents. My mother was Unitarian, my father was nothing. There was no religion in our house. My parents were of the mind that you're born, you live a noble life, you die.

"So when I found out about my roots, I felt some resonance with the culture but no need to adopt the Jewish faith. However, if I ever encountered people sounding anti-Semitic, and it's happened all too many times in my life, when pressed I'd say I was of The Tribe. Which usually just confused them.

"I guess you didn't need to hear all of that. But yes, I know about discrimination. And don't you for a minute think that I don't have a stake in fixing our education system. Without quality leaders, we risk another Holocaust. Maybe this time against intellectuals. I have taken leave from a job I love, I've left my home in Boston, to help Murray make the Bright Wise program into a success that will move us back from the brink."

Drew kept his eyes on Joan for a long moment, and then looked at Murray.

"I didn't know the details, Drew. I'm sorry about what happened to your forbears. Your roots, such as you have experienced them, have brought you here, and I am more than pleased that you are working with us."

Drew nodded to Stone. Stone stood up, announced that he needed some air, and looking at Drew, nodded toward the door. They picked up their papers and left them on Stone's desk before they walked out of the building.

"Have you been to the ocean yet?"

"Not yet this trip."

"I know a great beach," Stone offered, and walked over to his car. In fifteen minutes, they were parked off the road out past Asilomar. As they got out of the car, they both could feel the stress of the last part of the meeting leaving their bodies. The freedom grew as they walked a path down to the beach.

"This is like heaven to me, Drew. I try to walk here every day I'm in town, up the beach to China Rock and then back down here. About four miles, takes about 70 minutes walking, but sometimes I sit and watch the whales migrating in the winter, or flights of pelicans; they are such graceful birds, in the air."

"Sounds like a marvelous way to get your mind away from the cerebral."

Stone laughed. "It does that, for sure, or I go for a second loop." After a while he broke the ensuing silence. "I probably don't have to say this, to apologize for Joan. I was concerned when she was hired that she was stuck in the Sixties."

"No need to apologize, Murray. As you know, you meet many kinds in our journalist travails."

"Yes, but she is supposed to be colleague, if not on the same page then at least heading in the same direction. She's done this before, putting her left-wing dogma in the way of collaboration. There's nothing in your record that warrants anything but approval, for goodness sakes. Reading your pieces makes it clear that you wear a white hat." He chuckled. "I suppose she would have a problem with such a phrase. Anyway, I find that every time I'm in a room with her, I feel my defenses go up. I watch my words, and I don't like that. For me or any of the people I work with. I'm afraid she's going to have to go."

"Just so that it isn't on my account, Murray. It would be a helluva way to make an entrance."

"No kidding, but no. I think everyone has been aware of her issues since she started with us a month ago. She has made it a practice to be difficult with white males, and politically sisterly with the women and non-whites." He shook his head as if empty of its current thoughts. "No more on that. Mine to deal with and I'll do that later."

They walked on in silence, absorbing the salt air and the massaging sound of the waves. Suddenly Drew stopped, then did Stone who turned to look at him. "Murray, I have what may seem an oddball idea if you decide Joan needs to be replaced."

"I never arbitrarily rule out oddball, Drew, as you know. What are you thinking?"

"I know someone who is very bright, very conscious, and very much in touch with the needs of students."

"Go ahead. What would be oddball about that, considering our impending need for such a person?"

"He's eighteen."

Stone looked somewhat askance and then smiled. "Tell me more?"

And Drew did, about Michael Whyte. When he finished, clearly more enthused by the idea as he told what he knew of the young man, Stone looked at him and said, in all seriousness. "This could be our best appointment yet. And from what you say about his mother and grandmother, do you think they would support an early departure from Exeter to get involved in this program? What could possibly be as good an education as this work could offer?"

"I think the family and the school would be supportive, especially since he's gotten early admission to three Ivy League colleges and Stanford. Also, he could stay in the Boston area since there will be a school there."

"Amazing how the pieces fall into place, isn't it?"

"Providential," Drew agreed.

Chapter Thirty-Eight

It was early January, the dead of winter elsewhere, and Drew and Murray Stone were again feeling pacific, as they walked on the boardwalk above the beach and the Pacific Ocean in the warm sunshine that is the nation's other face of winter. Michael Whyte was contributing significantly in his role as a consultant to the identification of students, and teachers, to join the Bright Wise program. Funding and new commitments were coming in more quickly than had been anticipated.

"You'd be surprised at who is pouring money into their program," Stone enthused as they reached the beach. "I won't give you names but I'll give you a geography lesson. First, it's not Silicon Valley. While I have no doubt we could get money from some of the nabobs in social media and companies like Google, they were not the people who came forward on their own when they read my essay, which apparently was passed around in a big way.

"No, think about Wall Street, where some of the firms are looking to polish their image and need new thinking to get the job done. Think Hollywood where so much of the 'entertainment' they produce is facile and predictable. They are desperate for first-rate writers and new ideas. There were also people knocking on our door from the medical world, particularly the microbiology companies. They, too, need fresh thinking.

"And they are looking to us because they recognize that our approach to education will provide our students with both the story of where we are and how we got here, but also our graduates will have fresh minds, nurtured by our innovative program. The key to opening their minds is their understanding that it's not how well you do but how you do it well."

"That's an important story, Murray. Not only do you have a critical innovation in education, it is getting supporting recognition through innovative thinking in some of the older industries. That could easily shake some more money from the trees."

"That's what I was thinking. I can give you details and put you on the phone with some of these people who wish to remain anonymous for obvious reasons. It could make an interesting piece for the *Tribune* business section."

"Yes, that would get a lot of attention. And another way to get attention, Murray, I was thinking of applying my television news experience to interviewing some of the people in the company as well as new signed-up teachers, students, and parents. On camera. My guess is that you could edit those interviews to make some compelling videos to promote what you're doing, to attract more participants, and garner some quality news coverage."

"Drew, I think that's a great idea. I infer that you are parsing it this way because you're tiptoeing around the limits of your participation."

Drew laughed. "Yeah. I would like to be with you wholeheartedly, and I am in spirit, but for the coverage for the *Tribune* and the book to have validity, I have to remain above the proverbial fray."

"But certainly you could conduct the interviews for your articles and the book. That would only make sense. And we could select the sound bites to use. We wouldn't have to be bereft of your input, since you would be likely to use the best comments in your coverage."

"That would be reasonable, wouldn't it?"

"Transparently so, methinks. How do you want to start?"

"How about I give a call to Efram Marx and see if his wife and her partner, and their students might be interested?"

"You know, I think they would. Be more than interested. I expect they'd be downright excited."

"I'll call Efram when we go back."

Stone's attention was suddenly shifted away from work and he pointed out at the ocean. "Oh, Drew, did you see that spout? There's another one. Great. I love this time of year when the whales are migrating south. And they're in pretty close to shore, too. Amazing."

"Amazing it is," Drew replied, "We're watching whales spouting, walking by the ocean, in January and the temperature is pushing seventy degrees. I'd be happy here even if I didn't love my work."

Chapter Thirty-Nine

In a conference call with Allyson Whyte in Boston and Jeff Platen who was in Washington that morning, Drew traced a loose outline of what he had already learned and what he saw ahead.

"I'm planning on interviewing students, parents, and teachers, as well as the people managing the program. I have no question but that it will generate some interesting and informative content."

It didn't take the managing editor long to move the proverbial ball ahead. "We've talked about the *Tribune* videos, and upstairs wants to push them. They keep hearing from their friends that nobody reads anymore, they only watch videos." As an aside he said, "I hope they don't want to turn us into a cable news service." Then he went on, "Anyway, you've got a great background for this, Drew, with your work at ABC back when, so see about producing some videos about the program.

"I don't have to tell you that their call for doing the videos doesn't mean they're throwing a pile of money at it, but you know how to keep shooting costs from getting out of hand. Keep Allyson informed about what you're doing, and have her sign off on any that you think might stretch the budget, the one that no one has written down."

"Yes, sir."

"Anything in this vein scheduled?"

"There's been something of a Bright Wise pilot program in Seattle. Simulated classes for a month. Along the lines of what this full program is all about. Very successful. I was planning to go up there and use a local camera crew to tape interviews with students, parents, and teachers."

"Someone you know is going to do the shooting?"

"Actually, a fellow who shoots for one of the Seattle television stations. I met him a few years ago when I was researching a story up there. He's first-rate. Also, I found an excellent editor down here. They have already talked together about what I want and how I want it to look."

"Good. I guess I'm not surprised that you have your ducks lined up. Anything else?"

"If I might, one question. I would like to go with just the people associated with the program. I don't want to go outside for people who are opposed to it, for various reasons, especially the religious zealots."

"I don't like he said-she said reporting either, Drew. But you can raise the issues yourself, right, either in your copy or in your interviews?"

"That's what I intend to do, Jeff."

"Go for it. I know you're not going to proselytize."

"Praise the lord!" Drew said and they all laughed.

Chapter Forty

"Allyson, do you want to see a script first?"

"I'd rather see the piece when it's done."

"I thought you would. I should have it to you in the morning."

"That was fast."

"The interviews were some of the most concise I've ever done. People who know what they're talking about. And they know themselves. The children as well as the adults. What a world we could have if everyone was as conscious, at least, and mostly as bright."

There was a short silence and then Allyson asked carefully, "And you have this on tape?"

"The elements are all pulled. It's just a matter of assembly. You can see for yourself tomorrow."

"Amazing. Good. I look forward to it.

Drew had already finished writing his script, and gone through it with Jules Chen, the woman who was editing the piece. She hadn't suggested any changes, so now he was to record it. Jules set the audio board, and nodded to Drew. He shifted slightly forward toward the microphone and began.

The Bright Wise Solution

"Most of the talk about school reform over the past 45 years has been about tweaking the existing system rather than overhauling it. Increasingly, the reformers have been beset by opponents of change in general and their specific proposals in particular. In order to gain some degree of acceptance, those pushing for reform bowed to the ever louder dissidents, compromising the big ideas they started with into incremental adjustments that meant very little.

"But today, there is a new approach toward school reform and it is promoting wholesale change. Not micromanagement alternations but a major revamping of how we might educate America's children. Furthermore, the people behind this program have arrived on the scene with the resources – financial and human – to move their big ideas forward without requiring government or any civic group's approval.

"What they intend to prove is that education can be a wonderful experience for all concerned – students, parents, teachers, and the community – and most significantly, to have dramatically positive impact on our nation's future."

With that, Drew backed away from the microphone and waited for Jules to check the recording.

"Sounded fine, Drew. Good. You're a one-take wonder."

"Don't say that. You'll jinx me."

"I don't think so. You're not the type to lose his balance once you get started. Good thing. Okay, so I'll put in generic school shots over the top, and then what we shot of your people meeting in the conference room, and going over things together at their desks."

"Right. And next we'll put in the Selden sound cut. You have the transcript I marked up."

"Here it is:

Over the past several decades, America's public schools have been in serious decline. The last two generations have come through their K-through-12 system knowing less and less about the world they were entering. About the history of our great country, about the world, about the critical issues they are inheriting from the previous generation like over-population, climate change, militarism, health care...indeed, everything they need to know as they are picking up the reins of our future. If we don't make serious changes to how we educate the incoming adults, it is unlikely that western civilization will survive. Or that life on Earth as we know it will continue. It's that dire.

"Right. Then Murray Stone. I want you to cut together three pieces. The last one is short.

While the human race is on the brink, though many people think we can't come back, the truth is we can and we must. Our species – and particularly what is seen as a foundation spirit of our own country – is about coming from behind, pioneering new solutions to long-standing problems. We haven't been showing that indomitable spirit much since the end of the Second World War, but it's waiting to be reignited.

We have come up with a plan that will make some major changes in how our children are taught so that they can learn more and learn it better. And not just facts and concepts about where we've been and what we're supposed to know. They are going to learn more about who they themselves are, what makes them tick, what are their individual proclivities and their particular skills.

This is not pie in the sky dreaming. We have seen it work. And we know how to put it into practice on a wide scale.

"Now your second piece of track. And we're going to put up graphics over your copy." Drew nodded. Jules moved a slider on her audio board and started a new recording. "Rolling," she announced and gave Drew the cue to begin speaking.

"Stone is talking about upending the way we have taught in our schools for the past two hundred years. First, they are going to establish a national curriculum that begins with the three Rs and grows to cover all of the critical issues that a healthy-minded citizen in our democratic republic must understand at least in basic terms.

"Second, they will develop the individual student according to his and her individual interests and strengths.

"Third, they will do this in classes of twenty students, each class having two teachers and two teaching assistants to make sure that every student has the individual attention to progress in the direction that is right for them with the necessary guidance and support.

"Fourth, their school year will be expanded from the typical 180 days to 220 days, which is what schools in Japan and Europe have.

"Fifth, their courses won't run a full year but only as long as is practically needed to get the essential information across; in some cases weeks or months, though deeper issues like our American history will be covered over the length of the schooling to include contemporary issues and politics.

"Sixth, there will be three levels – Primary, Central, and Transitional – roughly comparable to first through fifth grades, sixth through nine, and tenth through twelfth.

"Seventh, students will be able to advance through the different subjects based on their own abilities and interests. They may be strong in math and move forward on it quickly, while literature may take more time for them to study and grasp.

"Eighth, students will learn basic life skills about civility, self-awareness, dignity, and truth. Later they will be instructed in home ec, and particular life-useful tasks like how to open a bank account and manage money.

"Ninth, there will be psychological and social studies to prepare the children to more effectively communicate and function in the adult world they are to enter.

"Tenth, they are starting with schools in three cities – Seattle, Minneapolis, and Boston – with only sixty students ranging through the three levels in each of the sites, with expectations of opening more schools six months later.

"And eleventh, they are accepting students based on their intelligence and their character, their ability to engage the educational process, and their potential, determined primarily through interviews with the students, their parents, and their teachers."

Jules looked up from her audio board and nodded her head. "I don't know how you managed that. Were you happy with the delivery?"

He smiled. "I think so," he said humbly. "Let's cut it and see how it works with the visuals. I can always re-track it if need be."

"Of course. Now we put in the sound cuts from the students, parents, and teachers, yes?"

"Yes. I gave you the transcripts and the tape times. Let's put them in this order. Use only first names and ages of the students and 'parent' or 'teacher' with the adults."

Robbie/6 years old - *My momma was my teacher and she really wanted me to be smart. And I wanted to be smart, for her and for me. And when I got to go to Bright Wise, I was so excited. There are other boys and girls who wanted to be smart, too. So we all pay attention and we are getting smart. So Momma can take a break.*

Reg/father - *Robbie wasn't right for public school. From the first day, I could see he didn't fit it in. He was bored, almost to tears. He already knew what the teacher was telling the other students. He started drawing – he loves to draw – but the teacher took away his notebook. School shouldn't be boring, ever.*

Monika/teacher - *It's so different from what we thought of as school. We have a collaboration with the students. We are learning together, expanding our minds, coming up with new directions, even solutions. It really goes back to evolution. The children come into life smarter than the previous generation. It's Nature's way. From what I've seen, when they go out into the world all grown up, they will know how to fix what the adults before them have broken.*

* * * * *

Cynthia/11 years old - *There was a time when I thought I wanted to be a teacher, but after junior high, where so many teachers had lost interest in teaching, I didn't know anymore. I like the people at Bright Wise much better, but I will decide what I'm going to do based on something that I learned there, about what Horace Mann said: "Be ashamed to die until you have won some victory for humanity." I believe everyone should think that way.*

The Bright Wise Solution

Alexi/mother - *It was like she came alive. Cynthia had been going to the local junior high school, getting top grades, but she had no energy when she came home. It was as though it was work for her to sit in class. But when we applied to have her go to the Bright Wise school, just coming home from the interview, she was a new person. The pilot has been great for her. She has blossomed there.*

William/teacher - *Our students are here to be engaged. They are purposeful, and demanding to be met; to be raised up, not talked down to. We take seriously the Buddhist philosophy that the best teachers know themselves to be students. It's a wonderfully regenerative process, for all concerned – the children, their families, we teachers, and the community.*

* * * * *

Sadie/12 years old - *My parents sent me to Catholic school for the seventh grade. But after one week, my parents were told to withdraw me. They said I was disruptive. That was because I challenged the nun who said climate change was a hoax, and then argued with the headmaster who said women shouldn't be accorded equal rights in the church.*

Nathan/10 years old - *I was hungry to learn, and excited to go to school, but my public school teachers were mostly just going through the same notes they had been using when they started teaching. It doesn't seem to matter to most of the teachers who their students are, except to keep attendance and give grades. My new school is so different. The teachers know who all the students are, as real people, and they make sure we understand what they're teaching us.*

Fiona/mother - *We have two children in Bright Wise, and they are doing so well. Finally, they are being inspired to learn, and they are thriving. It thrills my husband and me that these young human beings are growing into truly quality adults. Isn't that the best parents could possibly hope for?*

The Bright Wise Solution

Why, they may actually rescue us from the insanity of greed and war.

Isben/teacher - *This new approach to education has not only given me back my sense of purpose, that I can truly go about the critical task of preparing the next generation to take the reins of our society. It has restored my sense of hope about the children, at least those in my school. These young people are alive and have an appetite to succeed at life. And with what I've seen so far of the student-teacher relationship here at Bright Wise, we're going to turn out some very healthy young people who will lead very happy, productive lives.*

"Okay," Jules said, "And then we come back to your on-camera close-up we shot in the classroom yesterday."

"Yep, and that should do it, Jules," Drew said standing up and stretching. "I think I need a little sea air. I'll have my phone. Call if you bump into anything that needs a poke."

"Will do, Chief." She said these words having looked away from Drew; her eyes were on her editing screen. So she did not see him stop in his tracks, turn his head and stare at her. Nor did she see the broad smile that broke out on his face as he walked out of the editing room. She pressed a key, and Drew's closer appeared on the screen:

"These people you've heard from are clearly not your typical students, parents, or teachers. They are special. Some would call them elite, and in a derogatory tone. The implication is that by providing excellent education for the best and the brightest, as some might label them, we are detracting from those who are not so bright, not so skilled. Nothing could be further from the truth. The fact is that when we take the best students and give them the best education, everyone benefits.

The Bright Wise Solution

"By producing bright and wise men and women to move into influential positions in our society, we will be able to truly drain the swamp, as was once promised, and put healthy new leaders in government, business, health care, education, and other fields. We begin to restore the greatest of our nation's founding principles by producing the finest minds.

"This is the path that the Bright Wise group is pioneering.

"And note that not a single dollar is being taken from traditional public school funding. The money is coming from the parents, from foundations, and from corporations that are desperate for higher quality graduates.

"Note, too, that the Bright Wise people are publicly urging the federal government to shift funds from foreign military involvement to provide true national security here at home by teaching everyone in our country to read and write in English – the language of our Declaration of Independence and our Constitution – and do this by establishing free day and night ESL programs across the country. If we can't communicate, can't understand each other, there is suspicion and fear, and that erodes any feeling of security.

"Another major focus they are pushing for is the establishment of vocational training centers based on both the interests of the students and the needs of local business and industry. This training should be flexible so as to provide skilled workers for different fields as the need for them develops.

"The Bright Wise people also suggest that Washington revitalize a domestic peace corps to be a potential interim venue for those young people who are undecided about

The Bright Wise Solution

their future but who want to be active and productive while they are looking for something that fits their vision of what they want their lives to look like.

"That is our report on the Bright Wise Program. We will provide follow-up coverage of how their ideas are translating into reality over the coming year and beyond. In the meantime, you can get more information on their program online at BrightWiseSolution.com.

"Thank you for watching."

Jules sat back when the last edit was done. She checked her notes and then added a full-screen graphic which had the contact information for the program, and then the final screen with the *Tribune* logo and copyright text.

"Good job," she said to the screen.

Chapter Forty-One

"Good morning, Drew," Jeff Platen said. "I hope I'm not calling too early."

"No sir, I'm usually up with the sun."

"Like it there?"

"I do. Especially the weather. And no mosquitos."

"Glad you're enjoying yourself. But of course that's not why I called." This last was intoned in a more serious voice.

"Yes, sir."

"Upstairs screened your piece." He paused for effect.

"Ah," offered Drew.

"And they thought it was excellent," Jeff said with enthusiasm.

"Oh good. Thank you."

"Don't thank me, kid. You did the work. They did bring up one issue, and that was not having anyone on camera attacking the program."

"But..."

"But I told them of our conversation about he said-she said, and you would have loved it. They all exchanged

The Bright Wise Solution

glances with each other and soon they were all nodding their heads in agreement. I think they were surprised that they hadn't thought of the issue themselves."

"That's great."

"I thought so, too. Anyway, good job, they're happy, I'm happy. You are free to stay out there and keep reporting on the program. Come East when you want to or just need a break. I know Allyson would be pleased to see your face every so often. And stop in here when you do."

"Right, Jeff. Thank you again for all the support you have given me."

"Aw shucks, kid. Just doing my job. Take care." With that he disconnected the call.

A few minutes later the phone rang again.

"Hi, Allyson," Drew said upon reading the Caller ID. "I saw it's snowing in Boston. A lot."

"Aarrgghh, don't rub it in. I love living in the suburbs except when the people who can't drive in the snow take to the roads. But I didn't call to give you a traffic report."

"No."

"Jeff called, said he'd talked to you. Everyone in New York is very happy with your work, Drew. And so am I. Your report was top notch. Factual and poignant. You get an A-plus."

"Why thank you, Allyson. Last night when I sent you the link, I remembered our trip to Stockbridge to meet Laurence just after I moved to Boston. It was ages ago in terms of what's happened since, but only months in time. I can't tell you how much I appreciate you initiating what has brought me to where I am today."

"Back at you, Drew. You did the work. You must know that we are all very proud of you."

"And Michael is thriving."

"He is indeed." There was a brief silence and then Allyson said, "You know, I was concerned that he wasn't going to college, but he loves what he's doing and he's doing better than anyone could have imagined. I mean, he just turned 18, and he's producing like what we would expect from someone with ten years or more work experience."

It was Drew's turn to be silent. Allyson waited.

"Allyson, your son is proof of what young people – properly educated, guided, and nurtured – are capable of. It's clear proof that the goals of the Bright Wise program are reachable."

"Yes, I hadn't thought about it in those terms, even though it was right in front of my face every day – literally."

"He will be a chapter in the book, I think. Or maybe the preface."

"I don't know..." she said with reluctance.

"Don't make a decision now. I know you prize your privacy, but he is a marvelous person. You have done so well by him. When I start on the book, or maybe when I finish it, I'll write up what just flashed through my mind while we were talking and see how you feel about it. And Michael."

"I'm already warming to the idea, Drew. I think you're right." She paused. "When might we expect to see you on this coast. Are you going to wait until the snow melts?"

"That sounds like a good idea," he laughed. "Things are busy here, as you can imagine, but I'm planning on heading out there in late March, when there will be a break in the action."

"And most of the snow has melted."

He laughed again. "Thank you again, for backing all this."

"Be well, Drew. Bright and wise."

"Bright and wise, Allyson."

Appendix

This is the outline Murray Stone emailed to Drew Ekland which he read on the flight to Monterey.

The Bright Wise Program

To: Drew Ekland
From: Murray Stone
Re: Program outline

Here are some of the critical elements in the program for you to understand:

I. Primary focus on each student as an individual.
    A. A smorgasbord of choices of study
    B. Deepen self-awareness, define true inclinations, and identify skills
    C. Choose his initial path.

II. National curriculum
    A. Three Rs
    B. American history, global affairs, basic science, arts, literature, government, commerce, spiritualism, economics, the environment, criminal justice politics, et al
    C. Soft subjects; e.g., civility, dignity, and truth; home ec, self-healthcare, finances; etc.

III. Psychological and social issues
    A. Prepare students to function in society
    B. Understand character types
    C. Individual information processing styles
    D. Quality-Integrity-Purpose
       Respect-Compassion-Community
IV. School calendar
    A. Year 'round
    B. Four 11-week terms
       1. Vary subject time based on need
    C. Two weeks between sessions.
V. School structure
    A. Three classes
       1. Primary (ala 1st - 5th grades)
         5-year-olds; 6 hours/day
       2. Central (ala 6th - 9th grades)
         10-year-olds ; 7 hours/day
       3. Transitional (ala 10th - 12th grades)
         14-year-olds; 8 hours/day
       4. 20 students/2 teachers/2 assistants
       5. 15 administration and support staff
VI. Launch cities
    A. Boston, Minneapolis, Seattle

The Bright Wise Solution

About the Author

Tony Seton is a journalist, writer, and publisher. An Emmy award-winning broadcast journalist for ABC Television News, he covered Watergate, six elections, and five space shots. And he produced Dan Cordtz's business/economics coverage and Barbara Walters' news interviews.

Later, Tony wrote and produced two award-winning public television documentaries.

Through Seton Publishing, Tony has written, designed, and published more than 50 of his own books and screenplays, and has edited and published 30-some books for clients.

As a political consultant, his clients have included Nancy Pelosi, Tom Campbell, John Vasconcellos, the American Nurses Association, and various local candidates.

He has taught journalism and writing, provided media training, and produced websites.

Tony is also a private pilot and a photographer.

www.ingramcontent.com/pod-product-compliance
Lightning Source LLC
Chambersburg PA
CBHW061640040426
42446CB00010B/1516